THE SPIRITUAL... .. ..
TEILHARD DE CHARDIN

Robert Faricy was born in St Paul, Minnesota, and trained
originally as an engineer. Later he became a member of the
Society of Jesus, and was ordained in Lyon in 1962. It was
during his studies in France that he first became interested
in the ideas of Teilhard de Chardin. In 1966 he was
awarded a doctorate in theology by the Catholic University
of America.

Father Faricy is now Professor of Spiritual Theology at
the Pontifical Gregorian University, Rome, where he
teaches courses on prayer and on Christian social action to
priests studying for post-seminary degrees in theology.

He is the author of numerous articles and books
including *Teilhard de Chardin's Theology of the Christian in
the World, Building God's World, Spirituality for Religious
Life, Praying for Inner Healing* and *Praying*.

THE SPIRITUALITY OF
TEILHARD DE CHARDIN

Library of Congress Catalog Card Number: 81-51160
ISBN: 0-86683-608-X
Printed in the United States of America

5 4 3 2 1

Winston Press
430 Oak Grove
Minneapolis, Minnesota 55403

To

Mademoiselle Jeanne Mortier

CONTENTS

Contents

8

NOTE TO THE READER

The religious thought of Pierre Teilhard de Chardin – the Jesuit priest-scientist who, as his chief life-work, tried to reformulate Christian truths in contemporary thought patterns – was little known at the time of his death on Easter Day, 1955. Soon after, the publication of his philosophical and religious works began, and in the 1960s he was intellectually fashionable for his broadly scientific philosophy and because he had been persecuted by church authorities for his ideas. However, with the exception of one important book, *Le Milieu Divin*, his spiritual teaching as well as his theology of Jesus Christ remained largely unpublished and so unknown until into the 1970s, after the Teilhard fad had passed.

Today, serious scholarship, re-evaluating Teilhard de Chardin's contribution to Christian theology, finds that his real importance lies in his spirituality of Christian life in the world and centred on Jesus Christ risen. In this book, I have tried to examine Teilhard's spirituality thematically, presenting an overall synthesis and using unpublished material as well as his published essays and books. In particular, I have used Teilhard's personal spiritual notes, especially his retreat notebooks; these, unfortunately inaccessible to nearly everyone, including scholars, cast considerable light on his published religious ideas as well as on his own life and interior spiritual experience.

9

Note to the Reader

This explains the book's subtitle, 'Teilhard de Chardin's Spirituality'. The term 'spirituality' refers not only to written or spoken reflection on the Christian life as lived out, but also to that life itself. Spirituality is lived before it is formulated. Since the material drawn upon here includes personal notes from Teilhard's own interior life as well as his published writings, the word 'spirituality' seems appropriate, rather than, say, 'spiritual teaching' or 'spiritual theology'.

My aim in writing is to use Teilhard's spirituality so as to help the reader in his or her own spirituality. This book, then, can help the reader to reflect on his own experience of God, perhaps to formulate it a little better, and so to live it more fully and with greater awareness.

What importance has Pierre Teilhard de Chardin's spirituality today? In a fast-moving and sometimes confusing world, Teilhard de Chardin can help us to find a place to stand. He proposes that we stand face to face with Jesus Christ risen, and that we understand everything and everyone else in our world in terms of Jesus as Centre – as the Centre that gives meaning to, organizes, and sustains all our other relationships.

To anyone who looks for meaning in today's world, and for that meaning expressed in contemporary thought patterns, Teilhard has something to say. And to all who look for a God with a human face and a human heart, who can bring order and light and love into their lives, to all who look for a way of knowing and serving and loving God in and through the world, Teilhard can bring some help.

Teilhard de Chardin's ideas have, in fact, done this for me. I began to study his writings in 1961 when I was preparing for ordination to the priesthood. I realized almost immediately that Teilhard's religious experience, formulated in his writings, spoke to my own religious experience, helped me to formulate and understand my place in the world, my problems, my own relationship with God and his presence and apparent absence in my life.

At first I thought this was chiefly because of the similarities of our lives: both Jesuits – members of the Society of Jesus; both with scientific training, he as a geologist and I as an engineer. I know better now. Teilhard speaks to many people today, not only to Jesuits and not only to scientists, because his life experience so well mirrors the life experience of so many contemporary seekers after truth, lovers of humankind, searchers for a better world, and Christians trying to get their lives together.

Not so much that Teilhard was a prophet; rather, his life itself was prophetic in that it contained the stresses and conflicts that so many of us in these later generations experience. Born a century ago, in 1881, in a France that was lumbering out of the nineteenth century into the twentieth, moving from an industrial into a technological culture, losing the abstract God of the rationalists and looking blindly for a God with a face, Teilhard was a man of his time; even more, a man ahead of his own time and for ours.

His search for God and his love of the earth blossomed together into a vocation to be both a Jesuit priest and a geologist. And this twofold vocation grew over the years into a finding of God, in Jesus, in and through the world. Teilhard's writings show him groping towards God, his tentative steps in the direction of speaking the Christian message for himself and to the generations that would follow right after his. He made mistakes. His concepts were often clumsy. But his basic insights hold true, and they help.

This combination of sometimes clumsy groping together with the expression of greatly important basic truths for today can be found reflected in church teaching. In 1962, the Holy Office in Rome issued a warning, which of course still has validity, that Teilhard's ideas might for various reasons lead Christians into error. And at the same time, the Second Vatican Council was preparing its most revolutionary and most important statement, *The Pastoral Constitution on the Church in the Modern World*, a statement that shows clearly its grounding in the fundamental orientation and basic concepts of Teilhard's thought, which dominates the document.

In this small book, I have tried to bring that fundamental orientation and those basic insights to bear on our lives in this age. I pray that they help you.

I want to thank Lady Collins and Miss Lesley Walmsley for their encouragement and patience, Sister Lucy Rooney, S.N.D. and Jesuit Fathers Richard Hauser and Philip J. Rosato for reading and commenting on the manuscript, and Miss Leslie Wearne for typing it.

This book is dedicated to Mlle Jeanne Mortier.

Rome, 1980   ROBERT FARICY, S.J.

CHAPTER ONE

LOVE AND THE HEART OF JESUS

For Pierre Teilhard de Chardin, God does not stand aloof from the world, somehow at a distance, disinterested in the details. On the contrary, God has chosen to involve himself deeply and thoroughly in the world. God has become human, one of us; he has given us the greatest gift of all in Jesus Christ – himself. This mutuality between God and the world, the mutuality found in the person of the risen Jesus, is the centre of all Teilhard's spirituality.

God and the world come into synthesis in Jesus Christ; they are perfectly united in him. The whole of Teilhard de Chardin's spirituality swings on this one fact the way a vault door might swing on one jewel bearing. Doctrinally, of course, this one jewel bearing is the fact of the Incarnation of God in Jesus. But what lies behind it in the development of Teilhard's personal spiritual life? What form does Teilhard's faith in Jesus Christ take in his own personal history? What are the roots of his personal relationship with Jesus Christ, of his christology, and of his whole spirituality? These roots, as Teilhard admits to himself in his private journal in 1919, lie in the devotion to the Sacred Heart.

Although I never really analysed it before, it is in the Sacred Heart that the conjunction of the Divine and the cosmic has taken place . . . There lies the power that, from the beginning, has attracted me and conquered me . . . All the later development of my interior life has been nothing other than *the evolution of that seed.*[1]

The Sacred Heart in Teilhard's letters to his mother (*1915–17*)

The seed was planted by Teilhard's mother, as he recalls in the essay that stands as his spiritual autobiography, 'The Heart of Matter'.[2] He writes that his mother never tired of nourishing him on the devotion to the heart of Jesus, and that this devotion held the 'key and germinal' role for his whole spiritual development. The place of the heart of Jesus in Teilhard's life is perhaps nowhere more evident than in his letters to his mother. He writes about the Sacred Heart especially in the letters of the years 1914 to 1917, when he was at the same time laying the first foundations of the entire brilliantly original edifice of his religious thought. In 1916 he begins to put in essay form his insights into the relationship between God and the cosmos, a relationship in Jesus risen. The 'cosmic Christ' of his early essays is the Sacred Heart of his letters to his mother; and so it is not truly Christ who is 'cosmic' in those essays, but rather the cosmos that appears as 'Christic', for Jesus loses nothing of his human particularity in the essays, because Teilhard's own prayer life at the time of their writing is grounded in and centred on the Sacred Heart.

In 1915, Teilhard writes to his mother:

This is the time for each of us, and for all of us together, to let ourselves be governed by the desires of the Heart of Our Lord. It is necessary that, for life and for death, he find us ready for whatever he might want, and that nothing seem really desirable to us except to remain *united* to him, accepting what he sends, and acting according to his smallest wish.[3]

The accent, as in Teilhard's writings later, lies on love, action, and the will, rather than on truth, thinking, and the intellect. And, as it will be later in his writings, the reality of Jesus Christ is central.

Unshakeable confidence in Our Lord, for whatever he chooses, love of *his Will*, sought for its own sake as *coming from his Heart* and as our surest bond with him – I wish you that, *ma petite maman*.[4]

A letter a few months later anticipates to a remarkable degree his spiritual doctrine of *Le Milieu Divin*, to be written nine years later, and shows the roots of that teaching in Teilhard's attachment to the heart of Jesus.

Nothing equals a complete abandonment of the will to Our Lord. Nothing is more intimate to a person than his or her will, tastes, likes. To love and to look for those things in Our Lord is to *find what is most profound in him, his Heart*, and it is to meet him in a most sure and most profitable way. Most sure because nothing should be able to shake us at any moment from that true communion that God gives us in his action on us through every thing, every person, every event. Most profitable, equally – because everything in our life becomes material for supernatural growth, and because a thousand unpleasant realities *are* transfigured at the touch of God's always very loving hand.*⁵*

Teilhard finds, in Jesus' heart, the unity of his own life:

> In so far as one can see clearly what one is worth, I've found that the Sacred Heart has been good to me in giving me the single desire to be united with him in the totality of my life. I feel strong enough ambitions for the future; but, at the same time, I believe that I could easily give up all these projects if that's what God decided.⁶

He writes of 'communion with the desires of the Sacred Heart' and of how 'the love of the Sacred Heart' can become 'the best and only way of giving lustre to and transfiguring life'.⁷ He asks his mother to pray 'that the action of *Our Lord envelop me to such an extent and pass through me so much, that I do not see anything but him,* that I serve nothing except him, and that I serve him well in some way'.⁸ He adds, in the same letter, a remark that sums up much of his insight into the union of the world with God in Christ, and that indicates already his near-pantheistic grasp of how all creation holds together in Jesus Christ: 'In the measure that things pass, grow old, disappear, *the only true Substance of things, Our Lord and his Will,* appears better, and of such great value, don't you agree?'⁹

Love and the Heart of Jesus

The Heart of Jesus in Teilhard's journals (1939–54)

Over the years, Teilhard's expression of his understanding of the Sacred Heart changed as that understanding grew. The growth can be seen in the differences between his letters to his mother during the First World War and his spiritual notes during and after the Second World War. Moreover, Teilhard's prayerful attachment to the heart of the risen Jesus can best be seen in the notes of his annual retreats. For the seventh day of his 1939 retreat, he writes:

Seventh Day, 1st Friday (1 December 1939)

> *The Sacred Heart:* Instinctively and mysteriously for me, since my infancy: the *synthesis* of Love and Matter, of Person and Energy. From this there has gradually evolved in me the perception of Omega – the universal cohesion in unity.
>
> I would like to spread, effectively, this attraction (I do not want to say 'devotion', much too sentimental and too weak) to the universal Christ, to the *true* heart of Jesus.
>
> Clearly, my only reason (passion, taste) for life is concentrated, 'materialized', around the discovery (and therefore the manifestation and the promotion) of the *Universal Christ*.[10]

A year later, in his 1940 retreat, he writes: 'Sacred Heart – Personal Heart of the Cosmos'. This phrase sums up Teilhard's idea of the heart of Christ and of its place in the universal order of things. Just as the risen Jesus is the centre of everything, so his heart is the centre of the universe. 'The Sacred Heart is the Centre of Christ, who centres all on himself.'[11]

Not at all happy with what he perceives as the smallness and narrowness of much traditional devotion to the Sacred Heart, he finds fault with the official prayer of consecration to the Sacred Heart, and reacts to the prayer in the same words he uses for the encyclical on Christ the King: 'How static! how juridical! inferior to the teaching of [the Letter to the] Colossians!'[12]

The heart of Christ is the subject of retreat meditations, especially in the retreats from 1945 to 1950. In the 1948 retreat, he spends most of three days' meditation on the Sacred Heart, and refers to his private 'litany'.[13] This 'litany' was found, at his death, among the things on his desk, written on both sides of a picture of the Sacred Heart.[14] On the front of the picture is written: 'Jesus, the Heart of the world, the Essence and Motor of evolution.' On the back are several words and phrases referring to Jesus and to his heart, such as: 'Sacred Heart, Motor of evolution, heart of evolution', 'the altar of God, the Centre of Jesus', 'the heart of the heart of the world', and 'Heart of Jesus, Heart of Evolution, unite me to yourself.'[15] In his 1950 retreat, Teilhard devotes the sixth day to the Sacred Heart (he writes: 'Day spent, to spend, in the Sacred Heart') and the seventh to the heart of Mary.[16]

He found his own centre and strength in the heart of Christ; the journal entry for the sixth day of his 1945 retreat begins:

Yes, the vertigo of the fragility and of the instability; there remains the all-enveloping hand and the heart of

18

the Universal Christ. Come to me *one more time* on the changing and shifting waters; why do you fear, you of little faith?[17]

He finds the Spiritual Exercises of Ignatius Loyola – the basis for all his annual retreats – limited and confining. In particular, he writes of his own understanding of the fourth section ('week') of the Exercises as one that sees the risen Jesus in terms of the whole process of God's plan to move the world forward to the fullness of the pleroma, to the fullness of the fullness of all things in Christ; and he writes of a new understanding of the Sacred Heart in the context of this process.[18] Teilhard views the heart of Jesus not just as the centre of all hearts, but as the centre of all created reality, and especially as the loving centre of all love. He applies the words, in English, 'The Universal lover', to Jesus Christ.[19] A year later, he remarks: 'The irrefutable fact remains that the historical Christ appeared historically as the point around which universal human love is concentrated, condensed, crystallized . . .'[20]

Teilhard sums up his reflections on the heart of Jesus as the heart of the world in a few entries into the journal in which he kept notes of random ideas, notes from his reading, and ideas for essays. Two weeks before the feast of Christ the King in 1951, he writes that the theological problem is 'to find a heart for the world and to identify it with the heart of Christ'.[21] On the feast itself, he notes: 'The great secret, the great mystery, is this: there is a heart of the world (a fact of reflection), and this heart is the heart of Christ (a fact of revelation).'[22] He continues:

19

This secret, this mystery, has two levels:
– a centre of convergence (the universe converges towards a centre),
–a Christian centre (this centre is the Heart of Christ). Perhaps I am the only person who can say these words, but I feel that they express what every person and what every Christian feels already.[23]

Teilhard's journal notes, written only for himself, sketchy and laconic, nevertheless indicate not only an important side of Teilhard's own piety, but also something of the place of the heart of Jesus in the overall structure of his spirituality. In an essay written in 1940, just after the publication of the papal encyclical on Christ the King, Teilhard presents in a more theological and orderly form his views on devotion to the heart of Christ:

We can clearly distinguish a fundamental movement in the Church in the cult based on devotion to the heart of Jesus . . . clearly directed towards worship of Christ – of Christ considered in the ways in which he influences the whole mystical body, and in consequence, the whole human social organism; the love of Christ being seen as the energy in which all the chosen elements of creation are fused together without thereby being confused.[24]

It is, however, principally in an essay written shortly before his death, 'The Heart of Matter', that Teilhard writes about the heart of Jesus other than in private spiritual notes.

Love and the Heart of Jesus

'The Heart of Matter' (1950)

The purpose of 'The Heart of Matter' is to describe Teilhard's lifetime's inner psychological experience. He wants to reflect on his direct psychological experience enough to make it intelligible and communicable without losing its quality of having been lived. The essay is an effort to show how, during the course of his life, the world around him gradually seemed to catch fire until it became entirely luminous from within.[25] The key section of the essay consists of several pages on the place of the heart of Christ in his life.

The God of Teilhard's mother was the Word *Incarnate*, and it was through the humanity of Jesus, to which his mother introduced him, that Teilhard found a Centre for his world.[26] In particular, the devotion to the Sacred Heart served, in his childhood, to bring together his love for the world and his longing for an Absolute. It brought into synthesis the 'pagan' side of his self and the 'Christian' side by 'personalizing' the world through its being centred in the heart of Jesus and by 'Universalizing' God through understanding his love as radiating everywhere through the heart of Christ.[27] His attachment to the Sacred Heart, long before he had studied theology, had begun to synthesize in his own heart his 'upward' impulse towards God and his 'forward' impulse towards the world-in-evolution, towards progress, towards the future-to-be-built. And it is this continuous synthesis of the 'upward' and the 'forward' that sums up his whole lifetime's effort.[28]

From as early as he can remember, Teilhard writes, he never had any difficulty in addressing God as a Supreme

21

Someone; he always had a certain 'love for the Invisible One'.[29] This passion for God merged with his passion for the world, nourishing his love of the world and, in a sense, 'materializing' his love for God. This 'materialization' of Teilhard's religious sense found expression in his attachment to Jesus' humanity, and especially under the real symbol of Jesus' heart.[30]

The devotion to the Sacred Heart, although always implicit in the Church, had its beginnings – Teilhard reminds the reader – in seventeenth-century France, in a form that was ardent but curiously limited both as to its object ('reparation to the Sacred Heart') and as to its symbol (the heart of the Saviour considered in a narrowly anatomical manner). He adds that the traces of this double narrowness can be seen in this century in a liturgy that seems obsessed with sin and in a religious act 'at which one must learn to sigh without becoming overly irritated'.[31]

These negative aspects of the devotion to the Sacred Heart never touched the personal piety of Teilhard. Whereas the seventeenth-century devotion tended to isolate Jesus' heart in a closed-in sentimentality, Teilhard's own attachment to the Sacred Heart took the form of concentrating all the physical and spiritual reality of Christ in one definable object, his heart. It freed him because it enabled him to find a unity and a consistency in all of reality, because it showed him the absolute Centre of a changing world.[32]

Through the symbol of the Sacred Heart, the Divine, for Teilhard, took on the properties, the form, and the qualities of a Fire capable of transforming anything and everything through the power of its love-energy.[33] 'Christ, his Heart, a Fire, capable of penetrating

22

everything – and which, little by little, spreads everywhere.'[34]

Eventually, Teilhard's devotion to Jesus under the aspect of the Sacred Heart developed into an attachment to Christ-Omega. This development went hand in hand with his intellectual reflections, with the growth and refinement of his ideas. Not that Teilhard's devotion to the heart of Jesus grew less; on the contrary, it enlarged, grew in scope, as his understanding of the place of Jesus and of his love in the whole universal scheme of things broadened. Briefly, as he gradually elaborated his theory of evolutionary human progress he saw more and more that the risen Jesus whose heart he had always adored and placed at the centre of everything must be envisioned in an eschatological perspective. The risen Jesus must be seen as he-who-comes, as the goal of all history, as the future focal point of the convergence of all true human progress. As Omega, as the end-point of history's progress, in the ground of human hope in the future, Jesus is he in whom all things hold together from *up ahead*, from where he stands in the ultimate future, as the world's end, drawing all things to himself. But, precisely because the centre of the Centre of all things is the heart of Jesus, the energy that moves the world forward into the future and that unites persons around their personal Centre is love.

Love, human progress, and the Eucharist

It was well into the 1920s before Teilhard realized, intellectually, the implications of his own attraction to the heart of Christ for his theory of social evolution and for his spirituality. Before 1920, he has not yet even begun to reflect on the meaning of love towards a theory or a theology of love. He considers charity to be a unifying virtue, but a *static* one.[35] In his earliest essays, he laments that there as yet exists no adequate theology of love, and finds no philosophical basis for the precept of charity. Finally, with *Le Milieu Divin* in 1924, his views on love begin to take shape. Christian charity is the more or less conscious cohesion of souls that is engendered by their communal convergence in Christ. It is impossible to love Christ without loving others; it is impossible to love others in a spirit of human communion without moving nearer to Christ.[36]

From 1930 on, Teilhard works out a philosophy of love, analysing human love in the light of the world evolutionary process into the future. He describes love as the strongest, the most universal, and the most mysterious of cosmic energies. Essentially, it is the attraction of each element of the universe by the universal term of evolution, Omega; it is the primitive and universal psychic energy, existing at all levels of the universe. In its most rudimentary forms it is practically identical with molecular forces; later in the evolutionary process it takes the form of reproductive drives; in mankind, love has entered the realm of reflexive consciousness, of the spiritual.[37] In his analysis of human love, Teilhard examines sexual love, and then moves to the analysis of a love that he calls 'the human sense'. In its simplest form, 'the human sense' is found in the love of friendship; it can take the form of bonding based on dedication to a common cause or goal, the form of patriotism or of a sense of the oneness of mankind. Finally, Teilhard identifies a third kind of love, the love of the universe, a 'cosmic sense'. Ultimately and fundamentally, the 'cosmic sense', the love of the universe, is the basis for religion; in a world seen as in evolution, it is an attraction to Omega, the future endpoint of the world's history.[38] Teilhard pushes his psychological analysis to try to show that love is the basic human energy, the energy that carries humanity into the future. He also tries to show that only love can synthesize – unify – the actions of a person, the person himself, and, finally, all persons in one unified mankind.[39] The model for all this, as Teilhard admits, is Christianity. Christ considered in 'the full realism of his Incarnation' presents himself as a personal term of union in his Church, which in turn understands itself as a future-directed community of love.[40]

The question arises, of course: does it not seem that social totalization leads directly to spiritual retrogression and greater materialism?[41] If mankind, as it moves forward towards Omega, grows in unity, will not this unity lead to totalitarianism, to the unity of the antheap? Not so, answers Teilhard, if the unity is one of love. True union, union of heart and spirit, does not enslave nor in any way diminish the persons it unites. It *personalizes* them, helps them to grow as persons. In any domain of life, Teilhard writes, whether we speak about the cells of a body, the members of a society, or the elements of any synthesis, 'union differentiates'.[42] It is not *union* of persons that is the source of retrogression and materialism; true union of persons personalizes, develops the persons united. It is egoism, the opposite of going out to others in love towards union, that is retrogressive. Self-seeking ends in the reduction of self; paradoxically, the human person finds fulfilment only in

union with the 'other'. Only union through love and in
love (using the word 'love' in its widest and most real
sense of 'mutual internal affinity') brings persons
together not superficially but centre to centre; only this
kind of union can personalize the persons united.[43] The
law written on human hearts (Romans 2:15) is, basically,
the law of love. And, in the words of Norman Pittenger,
the destiny of every person, 'under God, is to become in
full realization the lover he was meant to be'.[44]

Finally, Teilhard fills out his general analysis of
human love by pointing out the necessity of some
existing autonomous centre that would be structurally
and functionally capable of inspiring and releasing
within mankind the necessary forces of love. Only a kind
of 'super-love' can synthesize all the earthly loves.
Without a really existing and personal centre of
universal coherence, there can be no true union of
mankind; this personal centre of love must be Someone
who draws mankind towards himself.[45] Is Christianity
justified in its claim to bind the rapidly converging
portions of mankind to the real and existing focal centre
of their convergence? 'If I were not convinced from
birth that this is so,' Teilhard responds, 'I think I should
ask myself the question.'[46] His philosophy of love has
become a sign that points to Christianity and that is open
to a faith-understanding of love.

In his 1940 retreat, Teilhard notes:

Into the famous text of Romans 8:38 . . . 'who will
separate us from the love Christ', I introduce a shade
of meaning that differs from Saint Paul's (even
though it follows his line). For Saint Paul, charity is
the force greater than all the forces; for me, it is the

dynamic milieu that embraces and super-animates them all.[47]

Christian charity is natural love elevated into the Christocentric zone of the universe where it manifests its astonishing power to transform everything.[48]

Love is the energy of evolution, and evolution itself is a universal forward movement converging on the risen Christ. Christian love, then, can and must include love of the universe; love in all its forms must be 'Christianized', brought into the zone of Christ.[49] Since all creation is moving towards Christ-Omega, the whole universe and everything in it is centred on Christ and charged with his presence. It is impossible to attach oneself to Jesus Christ without somehow entering into the true progress of the world. And, on the other hand, it is quite clear that we can make our way towards Christ and join with him only in the effort to complete and synthesize everything in him.[50]

What is more, the love of Christ can unite, synthesize, all our actions and our whole life. Since Christ, in virtue of his position as the Omega of the world, represents the focal point towards which and in which all things *converge*, therefore every operation, once it is directed towards Christ, takes on – without any change in its own nature – the character of a centre-to-centre relationship, of an act of love.[51]

In Teilhard de Chardin's Christian worldview, although the risen Jesus is Omega, the future apex of the cone of the convergent progress of mankind, this same risen Jesus is present now, in the midst of ongoing history. This presence is in and through the Eucharist. Teilhard's considerations on the Eucharist do not go

into the questions of how Christ is present in the
Eucharist (he takes the Real Presence completely for
granted), and of the relation of the Mass to the Cross.
His interest lies rather in reflecting on the dynamics of
the love of Christ present in and radiating out from the
Eucharist, and on what that means for the life of the
Christian and for the progress of the Christian community and of human society as a totality. He wants to
bring out the full depth and universality of the mystery
of the celebration of the Lord's Supper.

He writes that when Christ descends sacramentally
into each one of his faithful it is not simply in order to
commune with him; it is in order to join him physically
more closely to himself and to the rest of the faithful in a
growing world unity.[52] When, through the priest, Jesus
says the words, 'This is my body', those words reach out
far beyond the piece of bread over which they are
pronounced. They extend to the entire mystical body of
Christ, and reach out beyond the transubstantiated Host
to the universe itself which, century by century, is
gradually being transformed by the Incarnation. So,
from age to age, all the Masses in the world make up one
single Mass. And the true Host, the total Host, is the
universe continuously being more intimately penetrated
and vivified by Jesus Christ.[53] For Teilhard, one single
thing is being made in the unvierse, the total Christ, the
reconciliation of all things in Jesus.

It is true that when the words 'This is my body' are
said, 'this' refers primarily to the bread on the altar. But,
in an extended and secondary sense, the matter of the
sacrament of the Eucharist is the world itself. The centre
of Christ's personal energy is situated in the Host; but
the Host is like a blazing hearth from which flames

spread their radiance.[54] 'The world is the final and the real Host into which Christ gradually descends, until his time is fulfilled.'[55] Since the beginning of time, one phrase and one act have been filling the world: 'This is my body.'[56] Throughout the life of each person and the life of the Church and the history of the world there is only one Mass and one communion. Throughout history, a single event has been taking place in the world: the Incarnation, realized in each individual through the Eucharist.[57] In his last essay, written just before his death, Teilhard speaks of the extension to infinity of the eucharistic mystery itself – in a truly 'universal transubstantiation' where the words of consecration fall not only upon the sacrificial bread and wine, but also upon the totality of joys and sufferings brought about in the course of its progress by the convergence of the world.[58]

In the poetic essay 'Christ in the World of Matter', Teilhard describes three mystical experiences of a friend.[59] The first tells of gazing at a picture of the Sacred Heart; from the description, it seems to be the classical picture of Jesus offering his heart. The outlines of the figure melted away, and the power of the Sacred Heart filled the world. 'The entire universe was vibrant!'[60] The second and third experiences tell of how the 'friend' experienced the eucharistic Host, in a monstrance and, later, carried in a pyx, expanding in space and time to fill the cosmos. I have been told by one of Teilhard's oldest and closest companions that the 'friend' was really Teilhard, and that the experiences were true religious experiences of his own. These, and perhaps other similar graces of prayer, lie behind his theological and spiritual writings.

In his long prayer 'The Mass on the World', a prayer

he used himself when on geological expeditions and unable to say daily Mass, he associates intimately the Eucharist, the heart of Christ, and the idea of the risen Jesus as the Centre of the world. He prays, 'Lord, lock me in the deepest depths of your heart; and then, holding me there, burn me, purify me, set me on fire . . .'[61]

Teilhard finds the eschatological movement of Christianity in the polar tension between the presence of Jesus as Omega and the presence of Jesus in the Eucharist. The risen Christ stands as history's terminal point, drawing all things to himself through love. And the same Jesus Christ stands in history's midst in his eucharistic presence – not leaving his place in the ultimate future, but making that ultimate future present now as the ground of human hope. The eucharistic Jesus holds in his hands the future of each person and of the entire universe; present now, he makes the future inchoatively present so that hope in him is hope in the future. The work of the Jesus to whom we adhere in faith, and who gives us hope, is love. This love radiates from his heart, the heart of him-who-is-to-come present now, centred in the Eucharist, filling the world.

Prayer for the gift of love

Teilhard often found it difficult to love others, and this prayer from *Le Milieu Divin* admits his, and our, weakness and dependence on the power of the Lord's love for us in us.

Grant, O God, that the light of your countenance may

shine for me in . . . my brothers and sisters . . .

You do not ask for the psychologically impossible – since what I am asked to cherish in the vast and unknown crowd is never anything save one and the same personal being which is yours.

Nor do you call for any hypocritical protestations of love for my neighbour, because – since my heart cannot reach your person except at the depths of all that is most individually and concretely personal in every 'other' – it is to the 'other' *himself*, and not to some vague entity around him or her, that my love is addressed.

No, you do not ask anything false or unattainable of me. You merely, through your revelation and your grace, force what is most human in me to become conscious of itself at last. Humanity was sleeping – it is still sleeping – imprisoned in the narrow joys of its little closed loves . . .

Jesus, Saviour of human activity to which you have given meaning, Saviour of human suffering to which you have given living value, be also the Saviour of human unity; compel us to discard our pettinesses, and to venture forth, resting upon you, into the uncharted ocean of charity.[62]

CHAPTER TWO

ALL THINGS IN CHRIST

The spiritual theology of Pierre Teilhard de Chardin takes the form of a spirituality of conquest. This spirituality is based directly on Teilhard's christology. The aim of his christology is a contemporary understanding of the mystery of the relationship between God and the world; this relationship exists and holds together in Jesus Christ. Any Christian theology depends on two sources: divine revelation as contained in Scripture and as interpreted in the Christian tradition, and some kind of philosophy that can stand by itself – independent of divine revelation – and that serves as an instrument for understanding God's revelation to man. For example, St Thomas Aquinas interprets God's revelation to us in Christ as contained in Scripture and Christian tradition within the framework of the philosophy of Aristotle. St Augustine, in his theology, understands Christian revelation in the categories of neo-Platonic philosophy. So, too, Teilhard's theology is based on two sources: Scripture as taught in the tradition of the Church, and a systematic framework. His theology is a christology that is grounded immediately in the New Testament christologies of John's gospel and the letters of Paul; it is developed within the systematic framework of Teilhard's own theology of evolution.

Teilhard's thought, then, as he himself has pointed out, is in three stages.[1] The first stage is a theology of evolution that sees evolution as following an axis of increasing organization and of correlatively increasing consciousness; this evolution takes place, after the appearance of man, chiefly in the form of human progress. It is a convergent evolution that is headed towards a projected point of maximum human organization and consciousness, the Omega point. The apex of the cone of evolution is Omega. In the light of Christian revelation, Teilhard discovers the focal centre of the world's progress, the Omega of his theory of evolution, to be the risen Christ. This is the second level of Teilhard's thought, his christology. At a third level, Teilhard constructs a contemporary spirituality based on his theology of Christ. Thus, the structure of Teilhard de Chardin's religious thought is: a spirituality of union with God through the world, based on a Christocentric vision of reality that is developed in terms of a theory of convergent evolution.

Teilhard's spiritual doctrine governs the other two levels: christology and the theory of physical and social evolution. The main contemporary human problem, as Teilhard sees it, is spiritual, and so his christology and his evolutionary ideas point to his spirituality and in many ways are geared to it. This chapter takes up the development of Teilhard's spiritual teaching, and in particular Teilhard's view of the relationships between nature and grace, between faith in the world and faith in God, between matter and spirit.

All Things in Christ

The 'meaning of being human' and the 'meaning of being Christian'

In the period from 1918 to 1928, Teilhard's spiritual doctrine is clear, but the underlying vision has not yet been formulated in a completely coherent way. This is a preparatory period in many ways; the vision is rich and often poetic, but the vocabulary in which the vision is expressed is sometimes unstable and the concepts somewhat fuzzy. The spiritual problem of contemporary man is analysed and described in the important essays of 1911, 'Cosmic Life' and 'Mastery of the World and the Kingdom of God'.[2] Teilhard points out the necessity of a reconciliation between Christianity and the pursuit of progress in the world; a point of view must be found in which Christ and the cosmos are seen to be so related that union with one means union with the other, in such a way that a person cannot be fully Christian without being profoundly human.[3] Religion and earthly progress are compared to the summit and the base of a pyramid. They are distinct but intrinsically related, to be neither confused nor separated, mutually complementary; as the duality becomes more manifest, it becomes more urgent to make the synthesis.[4]

A decade later, in *Le Milieu Divin*, Teilhard states the problem more in terms of the personal life of the Christian as 'the problem of the sanctification of action'.[5] During this same early period, the Christocentric vision of reality is taking shape. It is a vision in which Christianity and progress, worship and involvement in the world, can be understood as in synthesis. But the problem is stated more clearly than

34

the cosmic vision. It is true, of course, that the teaching of *Le Milieu Divin* contains a spirituality that is consistent all through Teilhard's writings. But, at the time of the writing of *Le Milieu Divin*, the underlying vision had yet to be more clearly and more theologically enunciated. The vision is surely present, presented in the poetic prose of essays such as 'The Priest', '*Forma Christi*', and 'The Mass on the World'.[6] And the theological concepts are beginning to express that vision in an increasingly adequate way.

In the years 1929 to 1936, Teilhard concentrates to a great extent on the contemporary spiritual problem. In particular, he elaborates an analysis of what he names 'the religion of earth' and 'the meaning of being human' (*le sens humain*).[7] He points out that the chief religious problem of today is the lack of reasoned and lived synthesis between Christian faith and what is best in the modern spirit. The distinguishing characteristics of the contemporary spirit are a sense of the *universal* and a sense of the *future*. Man today has a sense of the universal that is a total view of the universe, and his sense of the future is a faith in the possibilities of progress. These two, a comprehensive view of reality and a faith, define a religion, the modern 'religion of earth'.[8] The 'mystique of the West' is a mysticism of construction and of conquest directed to the unification of the universe.[9] The problem is not that the world is growing less religious; in fact, it has never been more fervent. In a later essay, Teilhard writes that, although many say that religiously speaking the world is growing cold, in reality it has never been more aglow with heat. But it is a new fire which is beginning to take hold of the earth, a faith and a hope in a salvation associated with the

evolutionary fulfilment of the earth. The modern world
is not irreligious – far from it. It is simply that the
religious spirit is beginning to boil up and take a new
form.[10] For the first time in its history, Christianity is
confronted not with a major heresy, nor with a schism,
nor even with paganism; it is confronted with another
religion, 'the religion of earth'.[11] The 'meaning of being
Christian' is face to face with the 'meaning of being
human'. *Le sens chrétien* is confronted with *le sens
humain*.

The synthesis of the 'forward' and the 'upward'

In the period from 1936 to 1944, Teilhard moves from a
point of view that stresses the contemporary religious
problem to one that looks rather to the *solution*. This
time, which corresponds roughly to the beginnings and
the duration of the Second World War, is a time of
synthesis following the previous period of analysis.
Teilhard sees the solution to the modern religious
problem as beginning with a coherent vision of the
relationship between God and the world in the risen
Jesus, a relationship of unity in which the distinction
between God and the world is preserved but is not
deformed into a separation. The evolution of Teilhard's
thought during this period begins with a vision that
brings out what is common in the 'meaning of being
human' and the 'meaning of being Christian': the
emphasis on person and on spiritualization.[12] It moves
rapidly to the more highly Christocentric vision of
Teilhard's earlier writings, but now the centrality of the
risen Christ is expressed more explicitly and more

concisely.[13] The key spiritual insight of Teilhard's vision of the solution to the modern religious problem is crystallized during this period in two brief essays, 'The Awaited Word' (1940) and 'A Note on the Concept of Christian Perfection' (1942).[14] This insight concerns the relationship between nature and grace; it finds the principle of their relationship in the person of the risen Jesus.

What are human beings looking for today? What lies at the root of their confusion? The root of present-day confusion, Teilhard suggests, is that we have discovered the future as something greater than our present, as a sort of 'object of worship', as a new star. We necessarily feel the influence of this new star, and each of us has the problem of balancing three realities: the personal self, God, and the earthly future of the world that lies ahead. Teilhard wants to Christianize, to *Christify*, the new star, the future; he wants to see human progress as incorporated into the kingdom of God.

The way Teilhard finds to synthesize the three realities – self, God, future – is to begin by understanding them as in synthesis in Jesus Christ risen. Teilhard wants to see all things as together in the risen Christ, whom he calls the 'universal Christ' because all things hold together in him. The affirmation of a new Christian optimism in a universal Christ: this is 'the awaited word', the message that the world waits to hear the Church proclaim.

The second essay, on the Christian idea of 'perfection', although quite schematic, presents basically the same idea but in the language of traditional Catholic theology, in terms of 'nature' and 'grace'. Teilhard criticizes the traditional notion of the nature-grace

37

relationship, finding it inadequate. In particular, he rejects the idea 'that nature is completely finished', that nature is a static reality. Nature is far from finished, he writes; it is essentially dynamic and developing. The natural forces of man are still in full growth. Mankind is far from adult, far from fully created.[15]

Teilhard transforms the medieval idea of nature and places it in the perspective of a world in process. Nature, then, is understood not as 'being' but as 'becoming'.

Teilhard goes on to include in one overall concept not only human nature but all of nature; and so the interaction between man and the rest of nature – the interaction that constitutes human progress – becomes incorporated into the notion of 'nature'.[16]

Teilhard's understanding of the natural order and the order of grace is that they are in synthesis, and must be brought more into synthesis in Christian life. The medieval concept of nature, brought into the contemporary worldview, results in an understanding that seems to separate nature and grace and to make the ideal of Christian holiness one of fleeing from the world. But if Christ is he in whom all things hold together, the Lord of all powers, sovereignties, and dominions, who reconciles all things in himself, then the order of nature and the order of grace must be understood as in synthesis. The real reason, then, for Teilhard's rethinking of the relationship between nature and grace is the Christocentrism of his thought together with his evolutionary perspective.

It follows that the life of grace cannot be somehow lived out by flight from the natural or the material, nor even apart from the natural and the material. The way to full life is the way of Jesus, the way of incarnation in the natural and the material. Teilhard's principle is the Pauline idea of *kenosis* found in the Letter to the Philippians.[17] The way of Jesus was not to avoid the world but to become incarnate in it, to descend into the heart of the world so as to become, risen, the Heart of the world. The text with which Teilhard concludes 'A Note on the Concept of Christian Perfection' is *Descendit, ascendit, ut repleret omnia*: 'He has gone up; what does that mean except that he has also descended into the lower regions of Earth? And he who has ascended is the same as he who has risen above the heavens in order to fill all things.'[18] Just as Christ descended into the material world, so must the Christian, in imitation of Christ, 'descend into the world', involving himself in it. As Teilhard remarks, this is 'the very pattern of the Incarnation'.[19] To express this Christian 'descent into the world' Teilhard coins the word 'transmaterial' ('passing through matter').[20] Spirit no longer means 'antimaterial' or 'extramaterial'; it means 'transmaterial'. Spiritualization no longer means a break or a discord regarding the material; for Teilhard it means a working through the material.[21]

Teilhard's use of the notion of spirit as 'transmaterial' is in continuity with his theory of evolution. Evolution is seen as directed towards 'spirit' and 'person'. In the essay 'How I Believe', he writes that the unity of the world presents itself to our experience as the overall ascent towards some continually more spiritual state.[22] In this view of evolution as spiritualization, the distinction between matter and spirit is maintained, but there is no dichotomy between matter and spirit and no opposition between them. Matter is the proper vehicle of spirit; and evolution and progress consist in the always greater organization of matter so as to provide higher levels of spirit. Progress is a process of spiritualization.

In the same way, progress in grace can be understood as a progressive supernaturalization of the natural. In this way, the supernaturalization of the natural can be viewed as in continuity with, and as a part of, the whole process of spiritualization.

Progress in union with God is in and through matter; it is 'transmaterial'. Nevertheless, the emphasis is not on matter but on spirit. The primacy of the spirit is a consistent theme of Teilhard's writings, and it is in terms of spirit that he understands all progress. However, spirit is 'transmaterial', and the way of progress is through immersion in the material so as to emerge in the direction of spirit.

At the centre of this concept of Christian perfection is the idea of personal union with Jesus Christ. But the risen Christ, the 'God of the upward', is the 'God of the forward', the future focal centre of the whole movement of the world. Union with him, then, is a personal union that is in and through the world, a union in and through matter. The direction of Christian holiness is not away from matter but into it towards the risen Christ on whom the process of the spiritualization of matter converges. Personal relationship with Jesus Christ, the relationship at the basis of all lived Christianity, is a relationship in and through matter, in and through the world.

This insight is developed in later essays, especially from 1944 to Teilhard's death in 1955. During this last and most mature period of Teilhard's writings, he returns again to his analysis of the contemporary religious problem, deepening the analysis and clarifying the concepts. The problem is now understood in terms of the apparent divergence of faith in God and faith in the world. The fact is, Teilhard shows, that faith in God and faith in the world need each other. Teilhard's analysis of contemporary anxiety points out that the religion of earth cannot stand alone; by itself it is crippled. Its intrinsic flaw is that it cannot promise man an ultimately successful outcome to the present human enterprise; it cannot guarantee that something permanent will remain of man's present efforts. And the more man progresses, the clearer and the more anxious the question becomes: 'Where will all this end, and is it worth the effort, the labour, and the suffering?'[23]

At the same time, Christianity badly needs to incorporate the best elements of *le sens humain* of the 'religion of earth'. The defects are not in Christianity itself, but in the way it has been presented and understood. Christianity in our time seems to lack an essential quality – human faith and hope; without faith and hope in man and in man's efforts to build the world, any religion today will appear to be cold and lifeless, petty and small, and inadequate to man's aspirations.

There is, then, an intrinsic and necessary mutual complementarity between Christian faith and faith in man, in progress, in the world. In his clearest presentation of the problem and the need for synthesis between the two faiths, Teilhard writes that at the source of the modern religious crisis lies a conflict of faith, a conflict between man's upward impulse of worship and his forward impulse towards involvement in building the world.[24] The 'upward' and the 'forward' are, in reality, the two mutually complementary components of a complete Christianity; Christian faith is whole only when it is a synthesis of faith in God and faith in man.

During this same final and most mature period of Teilhard's reflection and writing, the Christocentric vision which is the basis of the solution to the problem and the underlying principle of Christian commitment to God in and through the world, becomes more schematic and even more focused on the Person of the risen Christ. Jesus risen is presented more and more clearly as the future focal centre of all evolution and progress, as he who gives to life its existence, its meaning, and its value. This is the universal Christ. It is, of course, the same Jesus of Nazareth, who lived and died and rose to become the personal Centre of the universe.

In a letter to the General of the Society of Jesus, near the end of his life, Teilhard puts the problem and its solution succinctly:

For the last forty years my attitude and my activities have been based on the threefold, ever stronger, conviction:

a. First, that (for many irresistible reasons) we have just entered historically a period of neo-humanism (characterized by the surmise, or even the acceptance as proved, that Man is far from having completed the biological curve of his growth – which means that he has not only a future in time, but also 'a future' to look forward to).

b. Secondly, that the conflict – only an apparent conflict – between this neo-humanism and the 'classic' formulation of Christianity is the underlying source of all today's religious disquiet.

c. Finally, that the synthesis *in Christo Jesu* between the ascensional force of traditional Christianity and the propulsive force of modern neo-humanism is what our world, albeit confusedly, looks to for its salvation (and the Society of Jesus, incidentally, has once again exactly the same role in this situation, but at a higher stage, as it had four hundred years ago when it was confronted by the Humanism of the Renaissance).[25]

Teilhard's personal relationship with Jesus Christ

Teilhard could write clearly and intelligently about the central religious or spiritual problem of our times because, in the first place, he lived that problem. It was for him, first of all, a personal problem. How to reconcile his love for his scientific work, for geological and palaeontological research, with his love for and conse-cration to God – that problem, in different forms at different periods of his life but always essentially the same problem, forms the backdrop of his own lived-out Christian life. But Teilhard did not live the problem so much as he lived its solution: to find all things, in synthesis, in the risen Christ.

What shape does this solution take in Teilhard's own life, and in particular in his personal prayer? The notes from his annual eight-day retreats reveal, in words never intended for eyes other than his own, and in an intimate and straightforward manner, how Teilhard understood and lived out his interpersonal union with God.

Like all members of the Society of Jesus, Teilhard

followed the Spiritual Exercises of Saint Ignatius Loyola for eight days every year. Teilhard always made this retreat alone and in silence. The last 'meditation' of the Ignatian Spiritual Exercises is called 'The Contemplation to Attain the Love of God'; it closes the retreat. Basically, it is a prayer to find God in all things so that the retreatant may love and serve him in all things. The reflections of the meditation aim at deepening the appreciation of the presence, the goodness, and the love of God in everything that exists; everything in the retreatant's life is viewed as a gift from God in which God himself is present for the retreatant, acting and working for him out of love.

In the four centuries since Ignatius Loyola wrote down 'The Contemplation to Attain the Love of God', Jesuits have commented innumerable times, in writing and in giving retreats to others, as to what Ignatius meant. The common interpretation understands the God of the meditation's title as the three Divine Persons in one Divine Nature, as God according to the ordinary Christian usage of the word. Teilhard has his own personal interpretation: 'God' here is Jesus Christ risen. And it seems possible that this was the understanding of Ignatius himself when he wrote and gave his Spiritual Exercises.

In Teilhard's 1922 retreat, in his notes for the eighth day, he considers the Contemplation as

> . . . a series of points of view: to discern in each thing: 1. the gift of God (the good God); 2. the reflection of God (God as beautiful); 3. the presence and the action of God (God present); 4. *God's unitive way* (Christ). The normal focus of this awareness: to be for God –

44

and also *to see* God-Omega.[26]

In later retreats, this conception becomes far more explicitly christological, and the whole Contemplation centres on the risen Jesus, on Christ-Omega. In the 1943 retreat, for example, Teilhard writes:

'Meditation to attain love' – that's it almost exactly. And yet, not really. Because an essentially true intuition of Omega does not yet have the physical-metaphysical categories in which it can find expression. It's a 'rough sketch of Omega'. The organic dimension is missing . . . And so, Saint Ignatius' text sheds light on how much we've changed in four hundred years.[27]

Teilhard is saying that Ignatius' Contemplation does centre on Christ risen as the Centre and focal point of all the rest of creation, but that the cultural thought forms of Ignatius' times limited him in his explanation.

In his retreat for 1945, Teilhard tries to understand 'the Contemplation to Attain Love' as the expression of a mystery that encompasses and yet remains distinct from the three great Christian mysteries of creation, incarnation, and redemption. 'Creation – *the generative aspect*; Incarnation – *the unitive aspect*; Redemption – *the laborious aspect*. And the synthesis, crowning these three: Pleromization.'[28] 'Pleromization', for Teilhard, means the process of the progressive unification and reconciliation of all things in the risen Christ. He wants to find Jesus risen in all things precisely in that they are in process towards Christ-Omega.

On the last page of his last retreat journal, for the final

day of the 1954 retreat, Teilhard has this entry: 'To be
united to Christ = to move everything towards union
with Omega.'[29]

'To move everything towards union with Omega'
sums up Teilhard de Chardin's Christian view of where
the world is headed, its direction, its teleology. The
phrase characterizes his ethics as well; the Christian is
called to co-operate with God's plan progressively to
unite all things in Christ. These ideas are central to
Teilhard's eschatology, the subject of the next chapter.

Prayer to Jesus, Lord and Centre of all things

During Easter Week of 1916, during World War One, at
Dunkirk, Teilhard wrote this prayer:

> Lord Jesus Christ, you truly contain within your
> gentleness, within your humanity, all the unyielding
> immensity and grandeur of the world.
>
> You the Centre at which all things meet and which
> stretches out over all things so as to draw them back
> into itself: I love you for the extensions of your body
> and soul to the farthest corners of creation through
> grace, through life, and through matter.
>
> Lord Jesus, you who are as gentle as the human
> heart, as fiery as the forces of nature, as intimate as life
> itself, you in whom I can melt away and with whom I
> must have mastery and freedom: I love you as a world,
> as *this* world which has captivated my heart . . .
>
> Lord Jesus, you are the centre towards which all
> things are moving.[30]

CHAPTER THREE

RECONCILED IN HIM

We live in a world where one finds injustice, grinding poverty, starvation, persecution, oppression – and sin, suffering, untimely death. Things are not as they ought to be. Christianity's answer to present difficulties is that there will come a time when every wrong will be righted and every tear wiped away, when things *will* be as they ought. Reflection in faith on this belief forms that part of theology called 'eschatology'.[1]

Teilhard's eschatology

Eschatology studies the polar tension between things-as-they-are and things-as-they-ought-to-be, between the present and the ultimate future. The religious thought of Pierre Teilhard de Chardin is fundamentally eschatological. Teilhard de Chardin's theology is future-oriented, worked out within the framework of a worldview that understands the importance of progress, of history, of building towards the future. As a result of this future-directedness, the central Christian mystery in Teilhard's writings is the *Parousia*, the second coming of Jesus Christ. For Teilhard, who thought in terms of growth and evolution, endings – terminal states of growth – are more important than beginnings. Naturally enough, the terminal point of the evolution of the world, the second coming of Christ, has a dominating position in the whole structure of his theology. It might be said that Teilhard sees the world and its progress from a projected point in the future. That point is the Parousia, the end of the world, the second coming of Christ.

Teilhard's eschatology, centred on the Parousia, attempts to formulate an answer to the problem of evil in the world in our time. We have lived with the terrors of the Second World War, of Nagasaki and Hiroshima, of the Nazi gas ovens, of obliteration bombing, with napalm and the gruesome confusion of the Vietnam war; we live with today's violent oppressions in Africa, Latin America, Eastern Europe, Asia. Today, problems of hunger have become famines in which hundreds of thousands of innocent people starve to death and the survivors carry permanent scars. Problems of political conflict have turned into wholesale repression, murder, and torture. Problems of business ethics have taken the shape of billion-dollar oil frauds and of depriving not some, but millions, of workers of their just wages. Homosexuality, no longer a mere deviation, has become a worldwide movement. Courts and parliaments ratify the killing of unborn human beings.

Christian thought's classical answers to the problem of evil leave us cold. Augustine, Aquinas, Scotus, and the theologians of the Council of Trent, did not live with our massive and wrenching knowledge of evil. They never heard a machine-gun; they did not watch a president's assassin assassinated; they never saw photographs of babies with hunger-bloated bellies and hollow eyes; they never dreamt of poisoned Kool-Aid for mass suicide.

On the other hand, in many ways the classical

description of the problem of evil still fits today. God is perfectly good and almighty, and evil exists. Therefore, granted God's perfect goodness, it seems that either he is not omnipotent because he cannot prevent the evil in the world (Manicheism, Henry James, some process theologians); or else evil is all in our minds, an illusion, merely the appearance of things (stoicism, Vedanta Hinduism, Christian Science). Given God's goodness, how does one reconcile his all-powerfulness with the reality of evil in the world?

In treating the problem at an intellectual level, Christian thinkers in the past have given their main attention to the question 'What *is* evil?' In general, the problem of evil for Christian thinkers has been the problem of *moral* evil. Even physical evil (suffering, death), for Christian thought, depends somehow on moral evil, on disordered will, on 'moral distance' or separation from God; this is part of the content of the dogma of original sin.

For Saint Augustine, evil is a privation of a good that a person should have, and results somehow from separation from God through sin. But why evil exists is a mystery. Why does an all-powerful good God allow human beings to do terrible things to one another, to sin? Could not God simply turn the human will always to do good? Augustine answers 'yes', but that God simply did not choose to so structure human existence. The human will, in its freedom, can freely choose evil as well as good. But the question remains, why does God permit this? For Augustine, the mystery lies precisely here, and our reason can go no further.[2] Like Augustine's, Thomas Aquinas' treatment of the problem of evil relies on metaphysical categories. Aquinas understands

49

evil as an absence of being that ought to be present.[3]

Evil as the privation of good due (Augustine), or of owed being (Aquinas), seems today woefully inadequate as a description of evil in our world. The reason/suggestion is this: contemporary culture, and so to a large extent contemporary theology, drifts free from its historically important metaphysical underpinnings and looks to pragmatic categories rather than to metaphysical ones. To describe and theologically to cope with evil today, a contemporary cultural framework must provide the grid on which to lay out the relevant data of Christian revelation so as to arrive at some coherent discussion of the problem of evil. We need a framework that is not metaphysical but, rather, teleological, prophetic, and even apocalyptic.

Teleological – for it has to take into account the fact that mankind today sees itself as headed into a future for which it finds itself responsible; and the problem of evil becomes a problem of responsibility for the direction of history, for the goal or *telos* of human society, for overcoming present evil and avoiding even worse in the future. Prophetic – because a Christian theological treatment of the problem of evil today has to *call* Christians forth to take that responsibility. Apocalyptic – because the apocalyptic dimensions of evil today demand an answer in terms of Christian apocalypse.

These three, the teleological, the prophetic, and the apocalyptic, are the three aspects or dimensions or, to be exact, modes of discourse of Christian eschatology. In both the Old and New Testaments, and in Christian tradition, as a whole, one finds all three ways of speaking eschatologically. In a future-oriented culture such as today's general Western culture, eschatology takes an important place in theological reflection. We can look at Teilhard's eschatology according to the three kinds of eschatological discourse: the teleological, the prophetic, and the apocalyptic.

The teleological aspect: overcoming evil in a goal-oriented world

The Old Testament most frequently expresses the teleological aspect, the 'goal-orientedness', of history in terms of the exodus. The exodus, more than an historical event, is a biblical category; history itself has the shape of an exodus towards the Day of the Lord. Just as the exodus had the promised land as *telos* or goal, so history has its own *telos*, is teleological. The genealogies in both the Old and New Testaments serve the purpose of underlining the linearity, the orientation of God's plan towards a promised future fulfilment.

In medieval theology, the lack of a strong historical perspective limits the human future to glory in heaven. Further, the lack of a strong historical dimension makes any theology of community difficult; a community necessarily is historical, with a tradition (past) and a commonly-held goal (future). Because medieval theology takes not an historical view but a metaphysical one, it sees man's significant future as primarily personal and as other-worldly. Human nature's *telos*, its destiny, eternal glory, exceeds human nature's grasp; therefore the need for grace. This is, of course, the nature-grace problematic that has dominated Catholic theology, most recently in the writings of Henri de Lubac and Karl

Rahner. Evil in this problematic is understood as lack of due being or good.

The traditional nature-grace framework is teleological. Once theology catches up with contemporary thought patterns and begins to think in categories of history, genesis, development, process, and evolution, the old nature-grace teleology drops from the centre of the theological picture and a new teleology takes its place together with a new understanding of evil. This new teleology emerges clearly in *Gaudium et spes*, Vatican II's *Pastoral Constitution on the Church in the Modern World*. The question of the human *telos* becomes, in *Gaudium et spes*, the question of the goal of history, of the future focal point of the whole human community. *Gaudium et spes* begins by describing the profound changes and the difficulties that go with these changes as 'the human race passes through a new stage in its history.'[4] The present crisis of growth has brought the world great problems, such as new forms of social and psychological slavery, and widespread hunger and poverty.[5] Present evils, partly the result of rapid changes, will be done away with when history reaches its goal and we find again 'all the good fruits of our nature and enterprise . . . freed of stain, burnished and transfigured'.[6] This goal is the risen Christ, 'the goal of human history, the focal point of the longings of history and of civilization, the centre of the human race . . . and the answer to all its yearnings'.[7]

Behind the Christocentric teleology of *Gaudium et spes* lies the theology of Pierre Teilhard de Chardin, clearly the most important influence, even a dominating one, on the document. Teilhard de Chardin's treatment of evil in the world is radically teleological; evil becomes at least partially understandable when the universe is seen as converging in an historical evolutionary process towards its ultimate goal, Jesus Christ risen and the final reconciliation of all things in him. The very fact of this convergent evolution towards the risen Christ means that evil is inevitable. For Teilhard, it is impossible that there not be some disorder or lack of organization in a multiplicity that is moving progressively towards a higher degree of unification.[8] Evil is 'the statistical necessity of disorder at the interior of a multitude undergoing organization'.[9]

In other words, the world's evolution converges towards a future focus, the risen Jesus; this evolutionary process is a progressive unification taking place through increasing organization, socialization, mass communications. In history, God draws all things towards himself, towards a unity in Christ. In a process of this kind, inevitably, every success is paid for by a certain amount of waste and failure. In non-living things, this waste takes the form of disharmony or decomposition. In living beings, it appears as suffering and death. And in the moral order, in the realm of human freedom, this waste and failure takes the form of sin. Evil, then, occurs by statistical necessity; there is no order in the process of formation that does not imply failure and disorder. In our world, writes Teilhard, 'evil appears necessarily and abundantly . . . not by accident (which would not much matter) but by the very structure of the system'; a universe in evolution is necessarily 'a universe which labours, which sins, which suffers'.[10]

Sin, then, is the free choice of disunion, of disorder. Free in each case, it occurs with statistical necessity for the whole human species moving gropingly towards

53

higher unity and higher organization. Evil in the world is the absence not of being or of good but of unity, of union. And sin is understood as the precise opposite of love, as anti-love; for love unites, chooses union; and sin separates, chooses disunion and disorder.

Teilhard's idea of evil as statistical inevitability in a forward-moving world makes original sin a transhistoric reality. Original sin exists everywhere and from the beginning; it is, simply, the inevitable existence of evil, a universal condition.[11] Teilhard de Chardin's theological hypothesis on original sin lies behind the Catholic wave of reflection on original sin in the 1960s, and has pushed theology to view original sin as universal, as widespread as the world, and in the shadow of the redemptive act of the Cross.[12] The redemption, in Teilhard's theology, compensates for 'statistical disorders'; it makes reparation for evil in the world.

The cold mechanicalness of Teilhard's idea of evil as the statistical necessity of disunion and disorder finds its balance in his conception of love as evil's opposite, triumphing through the Cross, unifying and creating new order through the merits of Jesus' suffering and death. Only the love of Jesus Christ, his love for us and our love for him and in him for one another, can truly unite with a force that overcomes evil in this world, with a bond stronger than mere human nature and that triumphs over this world's inevitable forces of disunion, of anti-love, of evil.

What has happened to the problem of evil as theology has cut itself loose from its moorings in metaphysical teleology and floated out into a process framework? For Teilhard in particular, and for Catholic theology in general, a vertical metaphysical perspective has given way to a more horizontal and historical view, and the problem of evil – now seen in terms of the *telos* not just of the person but of the world – has taken on new dimensions of community, of social progress and regress, of universality, and of relevance to the doctrine of original sin understood as the negative transhistoric condition of this world's reality.

And *love* has become more important theologically. In moving from metaphysics to process, theology has likewise moved from the intellectualism of Thomism and the neo-Thomisms to a neo-voluntarism that stresses will, action, and love as the response to evil in the world. In the light of this, it is not hard to understand the rise of the theology of liberation in the 1960s, partly an extension of the new Teilhard-influenced European theology, and partly in reaction against it.

The prophetic aspect: the call to responsibility

In the writings of Teilhard, the 'prophetic' element, the call to conversion to God and to responsibility in this world, takes the form of a Christian ethics of building towards the future, of an ethical imperative to involve oneself in the world in the direction of God's plan to reconcile all things in Christ. Teilhard formulates an ethics in the light of the ultimate future, in the light of the end of the world, the second coming of Christ, and the beginning of the world to come. It is a radically future-directed ethics and a prophetic call into the future. It depends on Teilhard's theology of the second coming of Christ, on his understanding of the Parousia.

All Things in Christ

The Parousia – that is, Christ's second coming, this world's end, and the beginning of the world to come – for Teilhard will come at the terminal point of human evolution. In this view, the end of the world is seen as a transformation of all things in Christ so that God will be all in all. The Parousia will mark not a gradual change but a leap brought about by divine intervention. There will be, nevertheless, a real continuity between this life and the life to come at the Parousia. Christ's second coming will bring about a renewal of the world, a renewal that will be a transformation. The world that man is building now will be the proximate matter for this transformation. Nothing that is truly constructive, that goes to building the world towards Christ's second coming, will be lost at the end and final transformation of the world as we know it. Human endeavour, then, has a permanent value, for it is a contribution to building the world towards its final transformation in Christ.

The evolution of the world towards the Parousia is, in a theological understanding of evolution, the expression of God's continuous creation, which is directed towards, aimed at, the fullness of the Pleroma, the final fullness of all things in Christ that will be accomplished at the Parousia. God's continuous creation of the world finds its expression in time and space in the process of the world's evolution, an evolution that converges on Christ-Omega and that will be fulfilled at the Parousia. Since evolution has become conscious in man, man can be a worker for the progress of evolution towards the fullness of the Pleroma. In fact, man's participation in evolution is essential if evolution – now conscious in man and taking place in the thinking part of the world –

is to achieve its purpose. Man himself is called upon to co-operate with God in the building up of the world towards the world's final transformation. Man is called upon to adhere to God's continuously creative action in the gradual formation of the Pleroma. Human endeavour is a participation in God's creative activity.

Teilhard's most developed reflection on man's participation in God's creative power is found in *Le Milieu Divin*. In his action, man, and in particular the Christian, adheres to the creative power of God so that one may say that he 'coincides' with that creative power; he becomes not only its instrument, but its living extension. The Christian is caught up in and joined to God's creative operation; the will to succeed in what he does and a certain enthusiastic delight in the work to be done form an integral part of his creaturely fidelity, of his obedience to the will of God. *What* we do, therefore, is important; it is a co-operation with God creating. The world and man's activity in the world have a religious value, a Christian value. And the faith of the Christian imposes on him the right and the duty to involve himself wholeheartedly in the things of the earth.

Teilhard often stresses that God is served and adored actively through creatures, in and through earthly activity itself. Worship of God, for Teilhard, does not mean to refer things to God and to sacrifice them to him. Worship means to give oneself to creative activity, joining that activity to God to bring the world to fulfilment by effort and research. The world is uncompleted, and heaven is attainable only through the completion of the world. The things of earth are not just 'instruments to be used to give God glory'; they are co-elements of the world, to be integrated by man in the progress of his work of the formation of the Pleroma through the building up of the world.[13]

Teilhard's ethic, as he often stresses, is dynamic, not static. It is a 'morality of movement'. 'The highest morality is henceforth that which will best develop the phenomenon of nature to its upper limits.'[14]

Gustavo Gutierrez has criticized Teilhard de Chardin's theology as too neutral politically: as concerned with the man-nature relationship in terms of science and religion, but insufficiently concerned with relationships in human society, with social, economic, and political relationships.[15] True, Teilhard, like *Gaudium et spes* and many European theologians, treats much the same content as Latin American liberation theology: human relationships in society, socialization, human progress, freedom and totalitarianism; but he does it with a certain political neutrality. The liberation theology of Latin America, and to various degrees the other liberation theologies (American black theology, African theology of liberation, theological reflection on women's roles), take properly political options. Latin American liberation theology – and I restrict myself here to that only – reflects on concrete problems, on Christian life lived in faith in specific (Latin American) circumstances. It aims not so much at truth as at truth-to-be-done, not at understanding only but at action. It comes closer to being spirituality than theology, and has even been classified as ideological rather than theological.[16]

Latin American liberation theology has developed particularly the theme of Christian liberation from sinful social, economic, and political structures. The biblical reference point is the exodus: God freed Israel from oppression.[17] Israel fell into another kind of slavery, but with hope, a hope fulfilled in Jesus who came to give his life that others might be freed.[18]

The freedom that Christianity brings is freedom from sin, and sin is often found in the very structures of human society as well as in the hearts of men. Sin within the person has consequences in society, and so it comes about that situations arise which are objectively sinful even though perhaps involving no subjective responsibility at the time that those situations exist. Sinful social, economic, and political structures do exist in human society; they are objective states of sin. Situations of unjust distribution of wealth, of oppression of various kinds, of homelessness, of starvation, of inhuman living conditions; these are all sinful situations, conditions of institutionalized violence.

Liberation theology tries to *call*, in the spirit of biblical prophecy, to take responsibility for changing sinful structures. It prophetically denounces social and economic injustice, in the concrete circumstances of Latin America, and it prophetically calls Christians to live their faith in the direction of liberating themselves and others from such sinful situations. The theology of liberation, therefore, calls to Christian love of a particular kind; a love of the poor and the oppressed, a solidarity of love with the suffering. The prophetic call to take responsibility for changing sinful structures is a call to take responsibility for one's neighbour, a call to sacrificing love. It is here that Latin American liberation theology finds its greatest dissimilarity to Marxist thought – in its motive force, which is Christian love. This love seeks identification with the oppressed poor, with those who, like Jesus did, die 'outside the walls', outside the *cives*, on the margins of civilization. It is a Christian love that takes the shape of service, a love that empties itself in imitation of Jesus' *kenosis*, and that, finally, takes the form of the cross.

In the past few years two important developments regarding liberation theology have taken place in the Catholic Church. In the first place, the post-Medellin enthusiasm has declined. Many of those engaged in the implementation of pastoral guidelines for liberation have become increasingly engaged in purely political activities that have little or no religious import; some ignore or reject the Church hierarchy. Some have carried liberation theology to a kind of extreme, mixing it with Marxism and putting it at the service of various leftist political movements such as 'Christians for Socialism'. And several Latin American bishops have had second thoughts about Medellin. Furthermore, hopes for liberation, for changing oppressive structures, have often been cruelly frustrated; there seems to be more real political repression in Latin America now than in the 1960s. And, even in the early months of his pontificate as well as in a marked way at the 1979 conference in Puebla, Mexico, Pope John Paul II signalled greater moderation for liberation theology and a return to the (to a great extent Teilhardian) principles of the Pastoral Constitution on the Church in the Modern World, *Gaudium et spes*.

The second development is the incorporation of much of what is best in liberation theology into the official teaching of the Church. In the autumn of 1971, the Synod of Bishops, in their document *On Justice in the World*, stated that economic, social, and political structures often oppress people, and the document stresses the need for the Church to denounce injustice, and not only to speak out but to act. Action for justice is underlined as an essential part of the Church's mission. The 1974 Synod of Bishops produced an official declaration emphasizing that the Church must promote 'the integral salvation of man, his full liberation'. It states further the need for church action to liberate men from unjust social and political conditions as well as from their personal sins and sinfulness. Finally, Pope Paul VI's document on evangelization, *Evangelium Nuntiandi* (1975), brings out many of the basic ideas of liberation theology.

Liberation theology has stressed the prophetic aspect of Christian eschatology: to denounce sin of all kinds and to fight against it. The weakness of liberation theology is that it almost totally neglects the teleological and the apocalyptic dimensions of eschatology; and in this it can learn from Teilhard de Chardin.

Because the theology of liberation lacks teleology, does not see clearly and explicitly an ultimate goal, it lacks any real theology of community – for a community defines itself not only in terms of its traditions but also in terms of its goals. Therefore, liberation theology lacks ecclesiology, a theology of the Church as community of service – and so the way is left open to give an ideology of liberation priority over church teaching.

Perhaps even more serious, theology of liberation has neglected the apocalyptic aspect of eschatological process, and so paid insufficient attention to personal relationship with Jesus Christ as victor over evil. And therefore it has not spoken enough about appealing to Christ for liberation, even though – in the Bible – liberation begins with crying out to the Lord.

Liberation theology has pointed to the exodus as a paradigm of liberation. But the exodus begins not with responsible action for liberation. It begins with crying out to God. The ancient cultic formula of Deuteronomy 26:5-10 contains a summary of the exodus experience in the form of a prayer of thanksgiving:

> And the Egyptians treated us harshly, and afflicted us, and laid upon us harsh bondage. Then we cried out to the Lord the God of our fathers, and the Lord heard our voice, and saw our affliction, our toil, and our oppression; and the Lord brought us out of Egypt with a mighty hand and an outstretched arm, with great terror, with signs and wonders; and he brought us into this place and gave us this land, a land flowing with milk and honey.

'Then we cried out to the Lord.' This phrase establishes the exodus as a response to prayer, to the cry of the people to God for help. The anguished cry to God for help constitutes a dimension of Israel's relationship with God and the beginning of Israel's liberation. Over and over in Israel's history, the people cry out to the Lord, and he hears them and sees their suffering and 'is moved to compassion by their groaning'.[19] Jeremiah's Lamentations, the Book of Job, the prayers of lament of Judith, Ezra, Nehemiah, Moses, Joshua, Gideon, David, are all examples of the crying out to the Lord that leads to the Lord's coming in power to liberate those who are suffering.

Jesus himself laments, quoting Psalm 23, 'My God, my God, why have you forsaken me?' And the answer to his prayer is the resurrection. The resurrection, as event, belongs primarily not to teleology nor to prophecy but to apocalyptic. And so does the whole idea of the liberating power of God over the evil that oppresses his children.

The apocalyptic aspect: the victorious Christ

Teilhard identifies Jesus Christ, the risen Lord who is coming at the end of history, as 'Omega' and as 'Christ-Omega'. In this way, Teilhard clearly indicates the apocalyptic aspect of his spirituality – by making central to his thought an image from the one thoroughly apocalyptic book of the New Testament, the Revelation of John. 'I am the Alpha and the Omega, says the Lord God, who is and who was and who is to come, the Almighty.'[20] 'I am the Alpha and the Omega, the first and the last, the beginning and the end.'[21]

What is apocalyptic? It differs from prophecy. Prophecy interprets the signs of the present time in order to point to the future. Teilhard's spirituality is prophetic in that it calls us to move with faith in the world centred on Christ into a future for which we are responsible. Prophecy calls us into the future that the prophet sees arising out of the present situation.

Apocalypse talks rather about the future that breaks into the present, about God's future for the world. Apocalyptic's message tells us that the future belongs to God. God is the Lord of history, in charge of the world. The Lord guarantees the future. Apocalyptic understands the ultimate future as depending on divine intervention, as belonging to God and to be brought about by him. God controls history, moving towards its final end and his final intervention. History has meaning; the world has purpose; the Lord himself will bring history to its final goal.

Teilhard's christology, then, is fundamentally apocalyptic. When he writes strictly at the level of reason, in a scientific-philosophical vein, not depending on Christian revelation, he sees the world as in evolution towards a final point, a goal. His perspective remains strongly teleological. But once he enters the area of theology, where reason and divine revelation meet, and begins to elaborate a christology, his thought becomes apocalyptic in many ways because now he is dealing with material that cannot be handled without an apocalyptic perspective.

Teilhard, like biblical apocalyptic, speaks of the future as God's. He wants somehow to communicate the hidden, the future-hidden-in-God-in-Christ. The future lies hidden in the Lord's hands because it belongs to him; he holds the future and makes it present now in a hidden and mysterious way through apocalypse (which means 'revelation' or 'unveiling'). Apocalyptic, then, uses images and symbols as the inevitably necessary vehicles for what remains by its nature mysterious and perceived only in symbol.

For example, the Bible uses legal metaphors for the final judgement. It speaks of the resurrection in an image ('resurrection' means 'to get up again', a 'rising up again', as when one gets out of bed in the morning) [22] because the future resurrection remains essentially hidden even though an object of faith. Even Jesus' resurrection, as transcending history in some way, belongs by its nature to the world to come.

The apocalyptic literature in the Bible – for example

the books of Daniel, Ezekiel (chapters 38 and 39), and Zechariah (chapters 12 to 14), as well as the New Testament Book of Revelation (the Apocalypse of John) and the apocalyptic statements of Jesus (Mark, chapter 13) – uses images and symbols and visions, sometimes exotic or bizarre or even grotesque, to express the message of apocalyptic. The mysterious 'son of man' figure of Daniel, chapter 7, finds an important use in the teaching of Jesus about the end of the world. The separation of sheep and goats symbolizes the last judgement. The Church becomes a woman clothed with the sun and with the moon at her feet.

The apocalyptic element in Teilhard's christology makes him use images, symbols. 'Omega' is the best example, and one of the many cases of his use of the image of the 'centre'. His theology of the world converging on Christ-Omega along the evolutionary axis of Christianity is basically speculation within the framework-image of a cone lying on its side with Omega as its apex. And the fundamental model of his christology is biological evolution. Some of Teilhard's most-quoted phrases use geometric or biological symbols to convey religious truth about the future hidden in Christ: 'Everything that rises must converge'; the 'God of the upward' and the 'God of the forward'; '*le coeur de la matière*' (an essay title that is also a pun – it can mean 'the heart of the matter' or 'the heart of matter').

If Teilhard's christology sometimes seems a little fuzzy, lacking the conceptual clarity he valued so much and strived for, it is because of the necessary apocalyptic dimension of what he writes about, and therefore of his writings. His teaching centres in a radical way on the risen Jesus coming in power at the end of this world, but

65

present already in his power and acting on the world and on our lives now. Teilhard gives primacy to the creative and saving power of Jesus risen who breaks into our present from the ultimate future, giving us hope grounded in him, consoling us and strengthening us. This is the apocalyptic genre, and there is just no way to fit that into neat conceptual boxes, no way to avoid images and symbols and a lack of sharp-edged clarity. There is no mathematics of love, no calculus of grace, and we see only darkly as in a poorly silvered mirror.

The Christ that Teilhard writes about is the same Jesus that he prays to, the risen Jesus of the apocalypse, powerful, consoling, saving in his power, breaking into the 'now' out of the ultimate future. In his notes from the fifth day of his 1939 retreat in Tientsin, China, he has three notations: 'Meditation: Matthew 25:31. The Judgement. N.B. Key verse of the gospel! "Son of Man" = Christ-Omega; cf. Colossians.'[23] On the last day of his retreat in Peking in 1944, Teilhard meditates on the Book of Revelation, chapters 20 and 21, and again on the second coming of Christ in Matthew's gospel. He writes: 'Shout to the theologians that this is exactly the idea that I have. Your Christ is too small! Let me make him larger – as big as the whole world (something that you theologians certainly do not see).'[24]

In fact, if the Christ of theology remains even today too small, it is partly because so many theologians continue to disdain the whole idea of apocalyptic and to use the term pejoratively (e.g. Gabriel Vahanian,[25] Harvey Cox,[26] Karl Rahner[27]). Only a few take the theological category of apocalyptic seriously (the best example is Wolfhart Pannenberg). Generally suppressed and disregarded by the theologians, Christian apocalyptic has surfaced particularly in fiction (e.g. Flannery O'Connor), in poetry (e.g. Gerard Manley Hopkins), in piety (e.g. devotion to Our Lady of Fatima), and recently in the theology of the charismatic renewal which understands the 'baptism in the Spirit' and the charisms as the power of eschatological Spirit breaking into the human present.

Does the apocalyptic aspect of Teilhard's spiritual theology detract from the value of human endeavour in building the world? Human initiative and effort are not only intact in Teilhard's teachings, but strongly stressed. The efforts and the fidelity of those who adhere to Christ are integrated into God's overall plan. In general, Christian apocalyptic never really detracts from the importance of human effort and human responsibility; the seven letters to the churches in John's apocalypse are a good example of this. And in Teilhard, too, the fact that history's goal is the definitive establishment of all things in Christ by a direct intervention of God does not diminish the value of human endeavour; on the contrary.

There remain two elements of Christian eschatology, and in particular of Christian apocalyptic, to which Teilhard gives little attention: the doctrine of hell, and the presence in the world of the Holy Spirit.

Teilhard, of course, accepts the doctrine of hell.[28] This belief does not, in his spirituality, lead to an ethic of fear because of the stress on love and on the universal loving influence of the risen Christ. Nor does acknowledgement of hell's existence lead to any Manichean temptation, because of Teilhard's strong emphasis on the universal dominion of Christ. On the contrary, hell, as an at least possible destination, makes human responsibility appear more clearly and makes the universal lordship of Jesus more awesome.

Why does Teilhard give so little attention to the Holy Spirit? Perhaps because the Holy Spirit's role has always been to manifest not himself but Jesus. The Spirit's mission in the Church is to bring to full stature the body of Christ. And his activity throughout the universe is to bring forth order and form, which theologians have always recognized as somehow revealing not the Spirit but the Son. The Spirit's energy is directed at revealing not himself but Jesus Christ, and so the Spirit, even when most active, remains hidden, anonymous.[29] So it does not seem entirely inappropriate that the Spirit remains hidden in Teilhard's thought and that Jesus alone is revealed and glorified. Even the energy of evolution, in general as well as in its form as love, both traditionally associated with the Holy Spirit, in Teilhard's thought points to Jesus and to the energizing force of his love.

Teilhard's eschatology, then, in spite of certain lacunae, balances the teleological, the prophetic, and the apocalyptic elements of Christian eschatology. His theory of evolution and even much of his theology – especially when he is speaking about Christ to un- believers – is teleological. His christology is also teleological but even more it is apocalyptic. And his spirituality calls us prophetically to unite in love with Jesus Christ risen, and in him with one another to take responsibility for the world he came to save.

Reconciled in Him

Prayer to Jesus Christ in the light of the revelation of the existence of hell

Nothing in Christian teaching could be more alien to Teilhard's natural temperament than the doctrine of hell, a doctrine that has always been a part of Christian eschatology. This prayer shows how he faced his difficulties with the doctrine, and how his acceptance of it deepened his appreciation of God's love and of human freedom.

You have told me, O God, to believe in hell. But you have forbidden me to hold with absolute certainty that any single person has been damned. I shall therefore make no attempt to consider the damned here, nor even to discover – by whatsoever means – whether there are any. I shall accept the existence of hell on your word, *as a structural element in the universe*, and I shall pray and meditate until that awe-inspiring thing appears to me as a strengthening and even blessed complement to the vision of your omnipresence which you have opened out to me . . .

The existence of hell does not destroy anything and does not spoil anything in the divine milieu whose progress all around me I have followed with delight. I can even feel, moreover, that it effects something great and new there. It adds an accent, a gravity, a contrast, a depth which would not exist without it. The peak can only be measured from the abyss which it crowns . . .

O Jesus, our splendidly beautiful and jealous Master, closing my eyes to what my human weakness

cannot as yet understand and therefore cannot bear –
that is to say, to the reality of the damned – I desire at
least to make the ever-present threat of damnation a
part of my habitual and practical vision of the world,
not in order to fear you, but in order to be more
intensely yours . . .

I pray, O Master, that the flames of hell may not
touch me nor any of those whom I love, and even that
they may never touch anyone (and I know, my God,
that you will forgive this bold prayer); but that, for
each and every one of us, their sombre glow may add,
together with all the abysses that they reveal, to the
blazing plenitude of the divine milieu.[30]

CHAPTER FOUR

BY HIS DEATH ON THE CROSS

Teilhard de Chardin's christology has as its centre the risen Christ especially in the mystery of his second coming. It is an eschatological christology that centres not so much on Jesus crucified as on Jesus risen who is the future focal point of all true progress. On this christology Teilhard builds a spiritual theology, a spirituality. This spirituality is the content of his greatest work, *Le Milieu Divin*.[1] It is a spiritual theology of the cross. It is true, of course, that the central axis of Teilhard's entire spiritual doctrine is the interpersonal relationship between the Christian and the risen Jesus; but this relationship is lived out by the Christian in and through the world. Just as Teilhard's christology is a theology of Jesus as he is now, risen, so his spirituality is a theolgoy of the Christian life as it is to be lived now, in this world. And, although Christ is risen, the Christian who is following him in this world is, as Christ was, in the existential structure of the cross. So, like any truly Christian spirituality, Teilhard's is a spirituality of the cross. Furthermore, because Teilhard's whole system of thought, beginning with his theory of evolution and including his christology, is ordered to his spirituality, and because his spirituality is dominated by the cross, it is – from this point of view – the cross that is central to his thought.

In this chapter, I will first briefly describe the place of the cross in Teilhard's christology. There will follow an outline of Teilhard's spiritual doctrine of the cross in Christian life. Finally, I will consider the role of the cross in Teilhard's understanding of death.

The cross of Jesus

Why, if God is good and loving, do death and hatred and violence exist? Why is there so much suffering, failure, pain, misunderstanding? Why is sinfulness part of the human condition? Christianity has always responded to these questions by saying that Jesus saves men from sin and death and, finally, from every evil; that there will be a time when 'there will be no more death, and no more mourning or sadness, for the world of the past will be finished';[2] and that man's suffering and death in this world are, or can be, somehow, a share in the suffering and death of Jesus.

The doctrine of the redemption has been formulated theologically in various ways according to diverse cultures. That is, at different times in the history of Christian thought, different models – conditioned by the cultures they existed in – were used to express and to explain the mystery of the redemption.

In early Christianity, the eastern fathers of the Church, Justin, Irenaeus, Origen, and later Athanasius, Basil, Gregory of Nyssa, and Gregory of Nazianzus, used the widely-spread and well-known institution of slavery as a cultural model. Man was a slave to sin and death. Jesus, through his death on the cross, paid the necessary ransom to free man from slavery to the powers of darkness. In the early Middle Ages, the cultural model of Roman law was dominant in the theology of redemption. Man has transgressed against God; the penalty for the crime must be proportionate both to the offence and to the dignity of the person offended. Only an infinite person can make satisfaction for man's sins. Much modern English Protestant theology has used the idea of Augustine, and later of Abelard, of 'moral influence': Jesus' passion and death move us to turn to God in conversion of heart.

Teilhard, too, uses a culturally conditioned model to present the mystery of Jesus' redemptive death. As early as 1929 Teilhard could see that Catholic theology of redemption, under the pressure of an emerging evolutionary worldview, was beginning to change.[3] He asks whether, to the informed eye, there is not already a barely perceptible change. Original sin is very gradually becoming understood as something more in the nature of a difficult beginning than a fall, the redemption more akin to a liberation than to a sacrifice, the cross more evocative of hard-won progress than of penitential expiation.[4] Teilhard's aim in using an evolutionary model to express the mystery of the cross is in no way to minimize the place of the cross in theology, but rather in order to underline the truth, the power, and the appeal of the cross.[5]

In Teilhard's theological vision, Jesus risen is the future focal point of the world's forward movement; the risen Christ is the goal of history and of all true progress. The world, then, is understood as in evolution, as in-the-making. The process of evolution, having produced man, is now – in man – conscious of itself; and it takes the form of human progress. Teilhard transposed the relationship between the world and Christ risen, as it is found in the letters of Saint Paul, so that the relationship

73

can be understood in terms of a future-oriented and evolutionary worldview that sees history, genesis, and development as essential dimensions of reality. It is a perspective in which the world is understood as holding together in Christ, as a world existing in Christ and depending on him for its very existence. It is not a static world, but a dynamic one, and it is moving towards a divinely fixed and proclaimed goal: the ultimate reconciliation of all things in Christ. Teilhard's faith vision of reality sees everything dependent on the risen Lord for its very being, and sees his influence in everything. To a great extent, this is the vision of Vatican II's Pastoral Constitution on the Church in the Modern World, *Gaudium et spes*, which depends in many ways on Teilhard's christology, especially in the introduction and the first section.

The risen Jesus, then, is the active focus of the world's convergence; and, further, he is the divine influence that pulls the world forward into the future and towards the final recapitulation of all things in himself. This helps to explain the importance of the Eucharist in Teilhard's christology. For the same Christ in whom the world holds together and towards whom it is moving is present in the Eucharist. In his real presence, Jesus makes present, in himself, and in an anticipatory way, the ultimate future of the world, and of each person – for he contains that ultimate future in himself. This is the basis for Teilhard's Christian optimism: that Jesus, who holds every man's future and the whole world's future in his hands, is present now in the world, in the Church, and in a special way in the Eucharist. Teilhard's optimism is not a blind faith in progress; he was well aware of the ambiguities of progress and the misuses of freedom. It is, rather, a hope in Jesus who has risen and gone ahead, but who is present.

But what is the place of the cross of Jesus in this understanding of the relationship between Christ and the world? In order to become the central element of the world, Christ had, first of all, to *be* an element of the world; and this, for Teilhard, is the fundamental reason for the Incarnation. Teilhard writes that for Christ to make his way into the world by any side road would be incomprehensible. The smallness of Jesus in the cradle, the even smaller forms that preceded his appearance among men, are more than a lesson in humility. They are the application of a law of birth and, following that, the sign of Christ's definitively taking possession of the world. It is because Jesus Christ was 'injected into' matter that he can no longer be dissociated from the growth of the spirit. He is so engrained in this world that he could be torn away from it only by rocking the foundations of the universe.[6]

In Teilhard's theology of Christ's redemptive depth, the cross of Jesus has two aspects. The negative aspect of Christ's redemptive work of the cross is reparation for evil, compensation for sinful disorder in the world. It is, however, the positive aspect of Christ's death on the cross that Teilhard stresses: the effort of reconciliation. By his death, Jesus reconciled, in principle and in a way that is being worked out in history, all things in himself; he reconciled the world with God, and the various elements of the world among themselves. It is this side of the redemptive act of the cross that is uppermost in Teilhard's thought: that Jesus, by his death, unified the world with God and within itself. The cross of Jesus is seen, then, above all as a work of unification. Jesus

Christ still bears the sins of the world. But, even more fundamentally, Christ structurally, in himself and for all of us, overcomes the resistance to unification offered by the multiple, the resistance to the rise of spirit inherent in matter. He bears the burden, constructionally inevitable, of every creation. Christ is the symbol and the sign-in-action of progress. The complete meaning of redemption is no longer to expiate; it is to surmount and conquer.[7]

In Teilhard's earliest written reference to the theology of the cross, in 1915, in his private wartime journal, he wrote: 'Evolution: *the suffering Christ* reveals to us its hard work and what it is like, and he helps us to carry the weight. And so the *cross* is brought into human becoming.'[8] A little later, in the same diary, he writes: 'The cross is the symbol of work more than of penance (the penance being in the work).'[9] This embryonic concept, scribbled in a notebook at the front during the First World War, takes fuller form thirty years later in the essays written just after the Second World War. Jesus suffering, without ceasing to be he who bears the sins of the world, indeed precisely as such, is he who bears and supports the weight of the world in evolution.[10] Jesus, with the world's sins, bears the whole weight of the world in progress.[11]

Why is it, if the cross has such an important place in Teilhard's christology, that he seems to attach so little importance to personal sin? It is true that Teilhard has a spiritual theology of the cross that is based on his theology of redemption, but where in all this is personal sin? It seems to be missing, at least for the most part. This is not because Teilhard was unaware of the importance of sin, nor because it did not, somehow, 'fit into his system'. Rather, Teilhard, in not underlining the importance of personal sin, was reacting to what he considered to be an over-emphasis on it in the Catholic tradition since the Middle Ages. His idea of sin is a realistic, quite unromantic, view: sin is simply evil at the level of human freedom. He did not stress sin because, as he writes in a letter to Father Gaston Fessard, 'I can hardly fail to see that the enormous penitential theory of Catholicism is an *hypertrophie* of a notion of evil – or even a slightly morbid distortion inclining the faithful to see only the dark and negative face of things.'[12]

The cross and Christian life

The cross of Jesus, the historical act of his suffering and death, was the reconciliation of all things in himself, the redemptive effort of uniting all things for himself. Therefore, the cross is the symbol not only of reparation for sin but, profoundly, of progress made in hard labour and suffering. Teilhard makes this clear in a letter late in his life:

> Decidedly, and making a play on words, one might say that at this time what is 'crucial' is the meaning of the cross: mere expiation? or, more broadly, expression-symbol of the 'evolutive effort' of spiritualization, with its two aspects of conquest and of suffering? I am convinced that it is only this 'second cross' that is capable of (and destined to be) the world's salvation.[13]

'The cross', Teilhard writes in his World War One journal, 'preaches and symbolizes the hard work of renunciation . . ., the cross is both the condition and the way of progress.'[14]

About the same time, in an early essay, Teilhard writes that the road our Saviour followed is the way of the cross that man is called on to follow with him.[15] Furthermore, because of the very nature of reality, the 'truth about our position in this world is that in it we are on a cross'; it is in Jesus crucified that 'every man can recognize his own true image'.[16] What is the meaning of the cross in the life of the Christian? Teilhard has two approaches to an answer to the question. At one level, he discusses the symbolism of the cross for today's Christian, what the cross as a symbol stands for. At another and more practical level, he describes the asceticism of the cross in daily life, and its place in progress towards greater union with God.

For Teilhard, the cross is the symbol of all real progress. It is 'the symbol not merely of the dark retrogressive side of the universe in genesis, but also, and even more, of its triumphant and luminous side.'[17] It is 'the symbol of progress and victory won through mistakes, disappointments, and hard work.'[18] Although over half the entire central section of the spiritual classic *Le Milieu Divin* is devoted to the spiritual theology of the cross in Christian life, there are a few pages where Teilhard writes precisely of the cross's symbolism. For example, the royal road of the cross is no more and no less than the road of human endeavour supernaturally righted and prolonged. 'Once we have fully grasped the meaning of the cross, we are no longer in danger of finding life sad and ugly. We shall simply have become more attentive to its barely comprehensible solemnity.'[19]

It might be thought that this view reduced the mystery of the cross, or at least its symbolism, to a simply natural place, but this would be an error. Here perhaps more than anywhere else in Teilhard's writings one finds the natural and the supernatural orders understood as completely distinct but as fully integrated. The cross stands not merely for human reality but, beyond that, for the assumption and integration by God in Jesus of all that is human. When Teilhard speaks of the cross, even as a symbol, he means the Christian cross; that is, Jesus crucified.[20] And he never reduces the mystery to mere symbolism, as though reality and symbol were separable. He concludes the section in *Le Milieu Divin* on the meaning of the cross by saying that Christ on the cross is both the symbol and the reality of the immense labour of the centuries which has, little by little, raised up the created spirit and brought it back to the depths of the divine milieu. 'The Christian is not asked to swoon in the shadow, but to climb in the light, of the cross.'[21]

For an understanding of Teilhard's theology of the cross, the most important of his essays is 'What the World is Looking for from the Church of God at This Moment: A Generalizing and Deepening of the Meaning of the Cross.'[22] This short essay is in the form of a plea to the Church to make clearer the meaning of the cross, to present the cross in such a way that it can be seen as the answer to man's aspirations. 'Christianity', Teilhard writes, 'is pledged to the cross and dominated by the sign of the cross, by its birth and for all time. It cannot remain itself except by identifying itself

ever more intensely with the essence of the cross.'[23]
But what is the essence of the cross, its true meaning?
In a letter to a friend a few years earlier, Teilhard had
written:

> The idea of a value of sacrifice and pain for the sake of
> sacrifice and pain itself (whereas the value of pain is
> simply to pay for some useful conquest!) is a
> dangerous (and very 'Protestant') perversion of the
> 'meaning of the cross' (the true meaning of the cross
> is: 'Towards progress through effort').[24]

In his essay on the meaning of the cross, Teilhard goes
on to point out that, even for Catholics, the cross has
been primarily a symbol of atonement and of expiation.
It has carried a whole complex of connotations and mean-
ings; among them may be distinguished three unfor-
tunate tendencies: a vision of the world as dominated by
evil and death, an attitude of mistrust towards man, and
a mistrust of the material. All this, of course, is secondary to the love of God for man, and to the love man is
called to have for the crucified Lord, both of which are,
more basically, what the cross stands for. But the
question is precisely here: how can that love be shown
not only without the quasi-Manichean connotations but
in a more true and, therefore, more appealing way? The
answer is, by restoring to the symbolism of the cross two
elements which belong to it properly: the transcendent
and the ultra-human (the supernatural) that man is
called to. This can be done, Teilhard goes on, by
understanding the cross as synthesizing these two: the
transcendent, the 'above', the 'upward' impulse of man
towards the worship of God; and the ultra-human, the

'up ahead', the 'forward' impulse of man towards building a better future. For this is what Jesus has done by his cross, and what man does by participating in the cross of Jesus: to raise up the world, to move it upward and forward, closer to God and closer to its own final point of maturation. The cross, then, must finally be seen and presented in terms of what it truly is: the act and the symbol of all real progress.

In the notes of his annual retreat in 1941, Teilhard writes that the cross should be understood in such a way that 'we can present it to the world with enthusiasm. It should (must) shock the loafers and egoists; it *should not* be a scandal for those at the forefront of human progress.'[25] Earlier in the same notes, after praying over the traditional Christian idea of suffering in union with Christ suffering, Teilhard writes: 'What a strange idea of the mystics and of piety: to suffer *because* Our Lord is suffering! But Our Lord is associated with suffering (is in suffering) precisely because he is the LOCUS and the beginning of total change [*renversement*].' He adds that true compassion is a participating in the *action* of the cross.[26] In a later retreat, he distinguishes two classic ways of making the 'Stations of the Cross': 'in compassion with Christ; and in compassion with all human suffering at the time (grief, anguish).'[27]

On the Good Friday just before his death on Easter Day, 1955, Teilhard wrote to his friend and provincial superior, Father Ravier, regarding the meaning of the cross:

The meaning of the cross – I have nothing substantial to add to the few pages I sent you in September 1952: 'What the World is Looking for from the Church of

God at This Moment: A Generalizing and Deepening of the Meaning of the Cross.'

What I thought when I wrote that (and when I wrote *Le Milieu Divin*) I am more convinced of now than ever. In a universe in progressive development . . . the cross (without losing its expiatory or compensating function) becomes the symbol and the expression of 'evolution' in its fullest sense . . .

And so, without attenuating the Christian tradition, it becomes possible to present to today's world the cross, not only as a 'consolation' for the world's miseries but as a 'stimulant' (the most complete and the most dynamic stimulant that exists) to make progress and to go as far as possible, on earth, for God . . .

Teilhard continues the letter complaining that at present even the most brilliant and penetrating contemporary Jesuit thinkers are still reflecting in a static rather than in a dynamic and evolutionary framework. He concludes:

But tomorrow . . . the crucified God (qua-crucified) will have become the spiritual mover the most powerful possible (because the most valorizing and the only 'amorizing') of ultra-humanization. This is my faith, that I would like to proclaim publicly before I die.[28]

Teilhard's ascetical theology is the translation into practical terms of what the cross symbolizes. This teaching is found in its fullest form in *Le Milieu Divin*. Summarized very briefly, it consists in three phases, or modes.

First of all, *centration*.[29] Man's first duty is to build and to find himself, to become himself, to grow as a person. 'First, develop yourself, Christianity says to the Christian.'[30] This is, of course, a lifetime programme: to develop personally, to unify one's ideas and feelings and behaviour, to grow in Christian maturity.

Secondly, *decentration*. This means that one cannot reach the limits of one's personal development, nor even arrive at anything like maturity of person, without going out of oneself and uniting with others. If you possess something, Jesus says in the Gospel, leave it and follow me.[31] 'Decentration' is Teilhard's one-word condensation of the gospel injunction to renunciation, to lose oneself for the sake of the kingdom so as to find oneself, just as the seed must fall into the ground in order to bear fruit. There exists in each man the elementary temptation that, in order to grow as a person, it is necessary to be egotistical, to be selfish, to work primarily for one's own fulfilment; it is the illusion that to be more means to possess more. But, Teilhard points out, we grow only by emerging from ourselves to unite with others.

Centration and *decentration* are not chronological steps but two phases of one dialectical process. They go together necessarily, and they lead into the third phase of Teilhard's dialectic movement of Christian perfection, *surcentration*, the subordination of man's life to a life greater than his own. This is the phase of union with God, of being centred not on oneself but on Christ. So, through *decentration*, through renunciation, man becomes less centred on himself and more centred on Christ as he shares in Christ's cross.

Centration, decentration, surcentration are, of course, the categories of the paschal mystery: life, death, resurrection. Just as the life of Jesus was a building towards the final decentration which was his death on the cross and was a passage to his risen life, so too the Christian's life is a continuous building and a fragmenting and a coming apart in order to come together again less centred on self and more centred on Jesus Christ. Christian life as a process towards holiness is, in its dialectical movement, a participation in the life, in the cross, and in the resurrection of Jesus.

Far from being an asceticism of flight from the world, Teilhard's spirituality of the cross is a programme of involvement in the world, a *kenosis* that is a way of the cross that leads to resurrection. In this perspective, even the most cloistered contemplative life can be seen as a profound involvement in the world because it is a radical *kenosis*, a plunge into the heart of the world in order to be as completely as possible centred on Christ who is the Heart of the world.

For Teilhard, then, there is no conflict between cross and involvement in the world; the two go together by nature of the very structure of reality. During Teilhard's lifetime, as well as after, this approach was neither understood nor appreciated by some of the best-known thinkers in the Church. Teilhard's correspondence with Maurice Blondel, in December 1919, shows anything but a meeting of minds on the relationship between attachment to human progress and Christian renunciation.[32] Less well known is Teilhard's public exchange with Gabriel Marcel in 1947. The great difference between the view of Teilhard and the Catholic existentialism of Marcel is clear from the following excerpt from the notes of the debate.

P. T. de Chardin: Man, in order to be man, must have humanly tried everything, to the end . . .

G. Marcel: That is an anti-Christian idea, and leads to Promethean man.

P. T. de Chardin: Man, if he reflects on what he is doing, finds himself led to perceive that he must go out of himself in order to attain the summit. What makes man Promethean is the refusal to go beyond his own action. Prometheus is trapped in a total death.

G. Marcel: The more man works in the direction that you indicate, the more he puts himself under conditions that make humility difficult.

P. T. de Chardin: We feel ourselves to be dependent on God all the more as we realize our weakness.

G. Marcel: If there is progress, then self-mastery has nothing to do with progress.

P. T. de Chardin: Self-mastery and the mastery of the world go together.[33]

This dialogue, although perhaps not easy to follow, needs no comment. It points up the originality of Teilhard's thinking as well as showing how far removed he was from the pessimism of post-World War Two European existentialism.

The cross and death

The emphasis in this chapter so far has been, as it is in Teilhard's books and essays and in his letters, on the positive aspect of the cross. Even though, particularly in *Le Milieu Divin*, that dimension of the cross which implies renunciation, diminishment, failure, and death, is often brought out eloquently and at length, in general Teilhard presents the positive aspect of the cross, the cross as the symbol and the reality of progress through suffering and hard labour. This is not usually the case in his private notes and particularly in his retreat notes.

In his own spiritual life, more and more as he grew older, Teilhard paid special attention to the negative side of the cross, and especially to the cross as the symbol of Christian death. In his earliest essays and private notes, he considers death with a certain scientific objectivity: in an evolutionary world, death is a law, the regular indispensable condition of the replacement of one individual by another.[34] At the same time, death is man's worst weakness and worst enemy, the sum of all the evils of the universe; it is the epitome and the common basis of everything that terrifies us,[35] and 'the form *par excellence* of the inevitable, menacing, newness-bringing Future'.[36]

Jesus, however, has transformed death by his own death on the cross. In itself, death is a stumbling-block.[37] But Christ has vanquished death. He has given it the value of a metamorphosis through which the world, with him, enters into God.[38] Christian death, then, is the final decentration.[39]

It is principally in the personal notes of his retreats that one finds Teilhard underlining the negative aspect of the cross, by which it stands for Christian death as a participation in the death of Christ. He made the Spiritual Exercises of Saint Ignatius Loyola for eight days every year; ordinarily, when making the Spiritual Exercises, one prays about death in the first of the four sections or phases of the exercises, the section treating of sorrow for sin. Teilhard, however, frequently – and always after his 1941 retreat – meditated on death in the third phase of the exercises, on the passion and death of Jesus. The meaning of the cross for him personally in his retreat notes is, above all, that it represents, and is, his own ageing and his forthcoming death, both as a share in the cross of Christ. This is the same spiritual theology of the cross that is found in Teilhard's published writings; it is the same cross that is the symbol of progress as well as the symbol of death. But it is this negative dimension rather than the positive that one finds Teilhard himself praying over in his retreats.[40]

Death, for Teilhard, opens out to the 'Unknown'.[41] He asks himself in his retreat journal: 'How is it that death does not kill, and in what measure truly does it kill, the taste for life? In fact, we live forgetting about death, and when death approaches, we lose the taste for life, or at least we risk losing it.'[42] He writes of the irreconcilability of death and action,[43] and of the double duty of docility to death and of a renewal of youthful spirits.[44]

Sometimes, the problem of his own anxiety in the face of death preoccupies Teilhard. In his sixtieth year, in the notes of his retreat, he records two anxiety-provoking questions regarding death: 'Will Jesus be there? Will he take me or reject me? I can fear the second possibility; yet, it should challenge and encourage me.'[45] A few years later, during another retreat, he writes that, 'in the last analysis, the only true suffering and trial is *doubt*; nothing would be hard *if* one were sure that there is a Jesus on the other side.'[46] And a year after that: 'As if Christ were *not* real for me. Should it be normal that Christ leave untouched the sensible surface of anguish and that he work more deeply, never at the level of what is felt and perceived but *beyond* it?'[47] In the retreats of the last ten years of his life, he writes of his 'vertigo of fragility, of instability',[48] of his 'physical anxiety',[49] and of the rise of the 'old fear: that there is Nothing on the other side'.[50] In Teilhard's later years his recurring and severe attacks of anxiety surely contributed to his fear of death. In a 1953 letter to his provincial superior, he writes: 'For the past month I've been going through a phase of anxiety – the kind that, several times since 1940, comes periodically and makes every effort I make extremely painful.'[51] And in a letter a few years earlier he writes: 'A surge of that nervous anxiety that is more or less my lot since birth (and that is picking up with age) has somewhat slowed me down.'[52]

The fear of death as a possible dead end is almost never absent from the meditation notes on death from Teilhard's last ten retreats. But the fear is on the surface; deeper, and expressed much more often and more strongly, is an unshakeable faith and trust in God. In 1944, Teilhard begins his retreat journal by writing: 'Alone in retreat; alone at death; God has to be faced centre to Centre, person to Person . . . *Usque ad senectatem et senium ne derelinquas me, Domine.* Certainly, from year to year, *advesperascit,* and quickly.'[53] The seventh day of the same retreat is set aside for meditation on the cross; and he writes:

> The difficult thing, in old age, is to accommodate oneself to the interior perspective of a life *without a future* for oneself. (Face to the wall.) And yet, so many immediate interests tend to evaporate . . . a superior interest is necessary to bind them together.[54]

In his 1945 retreat, he entitled the seventh day, 'Redemption, day of diminution undergone in communion', and makes this entry: 'To accept, to love, interior fragility, and age, with the shadows and the spaces ahead always shorter.'[55] In 1946, the notes for the day of meditation on the cross are brief: 'To love: Decline, and Life in spite of Decline; communion with Diminution *and*, with chance animated by the christic influence.'[56] The 1948 retreat speaks of 'communion through death'.[57] Finally, in his last retreat, in 1954, he notes: 'Seventh Day – Cross . . . Communion with: Senescence; Diminution. *Appropinquat hora Christi.*'[58] In the end, the dominating meaning of the cross is that it is a passage through death to Jesus Christ.

Prayer to the risen Lord to accept the cross in life and in death

Now that I have found the joy of utilizing all forms of growth to make you, or to let you, O God, grow in me, grant that I may willingly consent to this last phase of communion in the course of which I shall possess you by diminishing in you . . .

When the signs of age begin to mark my body (and still more when they touch my mind); when the ill that is to diminish me or carry me off strikes from without or is born within me; when the painful moment comes in which I suddenly awaken to the fact that I am ill or growing old; and above all at that last moment when I feel I am losing hold of myself and am absolutely passive within the hands of the great unknown forces that have formed me; in all those dark moments, O

God, grant that I may understand that it is you who are painfully parting the fibres of my being in order to penetrate to the very marrow of my substance and bear me away within yourself . . .

The more the future opens before me like some dizzy abyss or dark tunnel, the more confident I may be – if I venture forward on the strength of your word – of losing myself and surrendering myself in you, of being assimilated by your body, Jesus.

Teach me *to treat my death as an act of communion.*[59]

CHAPTER FIVE

THAT ALL MIGHT BE ONE

Pierre Teilhard de Chardin died on Easter Sunday, 1955, before the Second Vatican Council, before the publication of the vast majority of his spiritual writings, and before the post-Vatican II ecumenical surge. He lived and wrote in an age when ecumenism was hardly mentioned. Yet his spirituality is strongly ecumenical, with fidelity to his own Catholic tradition, openness to all forms of Christianity, and a realistic and warm outreaching to share visions with non-Christian religions.

Christian ecumenism

In these days there is much informal discussion of ecumenism among the Christian churches that seems negative, disappointed with the present state of affairs, uncertain as to the future of ecumenism. After the Second Vatican Council's *Decree on Ecumenism*, there was an upsurge of optimism and of activity, particularly on the part of Roman Catholics, with regard to work towards Christian unity. National and international theological dialogue groups were officially established; meetings large and small were held; ecumenical contacts were numerous and hopeful; Catholic secretariats for Christian unity were established by the Holy See and by national conferences of bishops. It was the bright, post-

Vatican II ecumenical world of open doors and windows, of mutual understanding and searching, of high if imprecise expectations.

The ecumenical structures have not changed; the dialogues go on; but now the hope often seems dimmed, the expectations pessimistic, the progress small. What happened? Where did the ecumenical *élan* go? Why do so many today speak, and realistically, of a crisis in ecumenism? What is the significance of the current ecumenical problem, of the present so-called crisis in ecumenism? And where do we go from here? The progress since the Council is solid and real, but is it finished? A brief study of Teilhard's principles of ecumenism can suggest some answers.

Since the Second Vatican Council, Christian understanding of the Church has developed considerably, and this is particularly true for Roman Catholics. For one thing, the Church is seen as including, somehow, all baptized Christians. The *Decree on Ecumenism* states that 'all those justified by faith through baptism are incorporated into Christ'.[1] The Christian Church, then, although divided, has a unity in Jesus Christ. And it is ecumenism's task to make this unity more real by overcoming divisions among Christians.

The Christian Church is understood more and more today, partly as a result of the influence of the ideas of Teilhard de Chardin, as a Church in process, in exodus in this world and moving into the future towards its ultimate fulfilment as the New Jerusalem in the world to come.

Teilhard understands the Church especially as the body of Christ.[2] Like any living body, the Church grows and develops, always remaining identical to itself. The

Church evolves in a continuous synthesis with human culture and according to its own nature as a body alive with the life of the Holy Spirit. The idea of the Church as an unchanging, primarily juridical monolith responsible for the handing down from generation to generation of a collection of immutable propositions seems gone for ever, and it seems doubtful that anyone could ever really have had such a static and triumphalistic view of the Church. The Church is not above or beyond history but incarnate in the world, subject to historical conditions; for it is the extension in time of the Incarnation. Like its founder, the Church grows in age and grace and wisdom.

Furthermore, the Church, the body of Christ, follows the laws of growth of living things, and – in a special way – the law that the price of progress is suffering. The Church is in the existential structure of the cross, groping and finding its way with the guidance of the Holy Spirit and with the assurance of God's promise, not the Church triumphant but the Church militant, in combat, wounded, suffering.

What is the relationship between the one Church that embraces all the baptized and the individual Christian churches? What is the relationship between the one and the many? And what is the relationship of the diverse forms of Christianity to one another? The understanding that one has of ecumenism among the Christian churches will depend greatly on how one answers these questions.

The answers suggested by Teilhard take the form of a theological hypothesis. Like any hypothesis, this one is tentative, subject to correction, revision, and development. And like any hypothesis, it will be true to the extent that it makes sense in the light of the available data and to the extent that it is productive of further theological reflection and of more enlightened and effective action. What Teilhard is aiming at, then, is a theological hypothesis that explains the relationships of the Christian churches to one another and to Christianity as a totality, a hypothesis that is as coherent as possible and that will be fruitful for ecumenical understanding and endeavour.

His point of view is that of the Roman Catholic faith. Theology is, as it has always been, faith seeking understanding. Since his Christian faith is Catholic, his hypothesis is presented within the framework of the teaching of the Catholic church. It might be objected that this is unecumenical, that a truly ecumenical theological hypothesis should take a generalized and overall Christian point of view. But there is no overall Christian point of view. The ecumenical problem is precisely that there are many Christian churches and as many forms that Christian faith takes. Ecumenical understanding cannot be advanced by the adoption by all of a general faith that would be the lowest common denominator. Fidelity to one's own tradition is a presupposition of any ecumenical dialogue. Differences must be faced honestly and either worked through – sometimes painfully – or simply accepted; the glossing over or the suppression of differences results only in superficiality, not in real understanding.

From a Catholic point of view, the central axis of Christianity is the Roman Catholic Church. Roman Catholicism is that zone of Christianity in which Christianity is found in its fullness. This does not mean that the fullness of Christianity is found *in an expressed way* in the Catholic church. Nor does it mean, of course, that the Catholic church does not grow and develop; far from being in its finished state, Catholicism itself sees itself as eschatological, as growing towards the fullness of its perfection in the world to come.[3] Nor does it mean that the Catholic church is the only true church, as though the other Christian churches did not possess Christian truth. And, further, it does not mean that the Catholic church cannot learn from other churches, that there are not elements of the Christian faith that might find a better existential expression in churches other than the Roman Catholic Church.

Evidently, all Christian churches possess Christian truth; and no expression of God's revelation to man in Jesus Christ will ever be perfect and complete in this world. That revelation is, basically, mysterious; we can know more and more about it, but never fully understand nor fully express it. What is more, all Christian churches possess Christian truth; and some of this truth might, at a particular moment of history, find more adequate forms of word and action in churches other than the Catholic church.

Yet, in the end, a fundamental faith presupposition of being a Catholic is that, among all the Christian churches, Christianity has its best expression in the sacraments and the teaching of Roman Catholicism. Teilhard de Chardin writes: 'To be a Catholic is the only way to be fully and utterly a Christian.'[4] And again: 'Speaking as a Catholic, I should have to say that if the Church is not to be false to herself, then (without any arrogance but by structural necessity) she *cannot but* regard herself as the *very axis* of Christianity.'[5]

95

The central zone, the central axis, of the evolution of Christianity towards the end-time is, then, from a Catholic point of view, the Catholic church. And so Roman Catholicism is, structurally, the central line, or axis, of ecumenical progress; the other Christian churches are, as it were, grouped around that central axis.[6]

If this is true, what can it mean to hope for and to work for Christian unity?

Lukas Vischer has written:

The differences between the various concepts of unity must not be exaggerated. In many respects there is a consensus. All churches assume, for instance, that unity has already been given in Christ. All agree that unity does not mean uniformity and that it not only permits but positively requires great diversity.[7]

This diversity among the Christian churches is one of faith, but the diversity of faith is institutionalized. That is, each Christian church has an institutional organization that incarnates its own form of Christian faith and that is the expression of its faith. Diversity of belief is reflected in diversity of institutional structures.

Is this institutional diversity, seen in diversity of sacramental systems and of church organization, destined to disappear somehow as Christians become more unified? No. On the contrary. Institutional diversity will be accentuated as the ecumenical movement progresses and as greater Christian unity is achieved. This is an application of a basic principle, perhaps the most basic, of Teilhard's thought. The principle calls for some explanation.

The principle is: *true union always differentiates the elements that are united.*[8] In the case of cells that are united to form a living body, or in the case of the members of a society, or in the case of an association of groups, true union does not confuse the elements united; rather, it differentiates them. The players in a football team are differentiated according to their positions in the team. On any team, for example a teaching team or a surgical team, the members are differentiated according to their functions. When the union is at a more personal level, as in the case of friendship, the union of persons differentiates the persons united; it personalizes them. This is above all true of marriage. To the extent that a marriage is a happy and successful union based on love and sacrifice, the husband and wife grow as persons. Each achieves his or her own personal growth not in spite of the daily lived-out marriage union, but partly because of it. The most sublime example of differentiating union of persons is the Trinity. Father, Son, and Holy Spirit are infinitely united in one divine nature; and they are infinitely distinct as persons.

In the case of groups, the same principle that union differentiates finds an application. When Christian churches grow closer to one another in unity, and when that unity is a true union in the love of Christ, then the individual churches do not lose their ecclesial identities, nor even become diminished in their own Christian particularity. The opposite happens. Each church becomes more itself, not in spite of the union, but because of it. True union or unity of Christian churches, a union in Christ, will – as it progresses – not at all reduce the institutional individuality of the churches; it will enhance that individuality. Each church will become not less itself but more itself, more faithful to its own tradition and to its own identity.

This is Teilhard's basic ecumenical principle for the Christian churches. In a short note, apparently written only for himself, he writes of the 'Christian current' in which 'a God of tension and love is the consummation of all personalization and all determination, as the centre of universal concentration.'[9] That is, the Christian God is personal, a God of love, loving and helping to love, and so – in Christ – God acts as a centre of universal reconciliation. And he is a 'God of tension', of the eschatological tension between present and ultimate future, between 'already' and 'not yet'; he is a God who pulls us into the future.

And so the Christian churches converge on Jesus risen who draws them to himself from – as it were – his vantage point at the future focal point of their convergence on him. If Christianity can be imagined as a cone then, for Teilhard, the axis is the Roman Catholic Church, the apex is Christ risen, and all the various Christian churches are phyla converging on the apex, Christ, around a central phylum, Roman Catholicism.

Notice, however, that Teilhard's model, as always, is biological evolution. He is thinking of Christianity as the body of Christ as an *organized* body. Therefore, it is precisely as organizations, as institutions, that Christian churches converge ecumenically. Contemporary examples of this convergence are the World Council of Churches, and national councils of churches – some of which include representatives of the Roman Catholic Church.

What form can the union of Christian churches, as

institutions, take? As it is doing now, union of institutional churches will take the form of associations of churches. Examples are confederations of churches that are similar to one another, and federations of churches that share the same tradition. This, then, is the present and future direction of the unity of churches as institutions. It is a direction of convergence; as churches group themselves together more in inter-church associations, they will become more united while at the same time becoming more differentiated, each achieving better its own particular identity not in spite of but because of its growing union with other churches.

In one of Teilhard's journals in which he kept notes of ideas for future reflection, he has an entry in 1954 that reads: 'Relationships: ecumenism (common ground versus axis of convergence)'.[10] The apparent meaning is that Teilhard wants to remind himself to think about the relationships between two different ecumenical points of view. The first is the 'common ground' mentality; ecumenism consists in the Christian churches finding their common ground, the beliefs and practices that they have in common, and uniting on the basis of these commonalities. The second point of view is that of institutional convergence.

Although Teilhard's characteristic perspective is that of institutional convergence in differentiating union, he does not exclude what he calls 'common ground' ecumenism. We can suppose that he would look with favour on the 'common ground' ecumenical initiatives that have spread since his death in 1955, initiatives such as different kinds of common worship and ecumenical prayer meetings, co-operation in seminary training, working on ecumenical social service and educational teams. But he would be firmly opposed to 'common denominator' ecumenism, to any watering down of the beliefs or the pastoral practices of the churches.

Eastern and Western spiritualities

In the same short essay, 'Ecumenism', in which Teilhard states his formula for Christian ecumenism, he treats at somewhat greater length the problem of ecumenical relationships with other religions and in particular with the Eastern religions. Here, Teilhard sees only limited ecumenical possibilities. The two great mystical currents of today, he writes, are not immediately reconcilable. The 'Eastern current' seems to flow in the opposite direction from the 'Western-Christian current'.[11]

Teilhard takes up the problem of Christianity and the other great religions, particularly those of the East, in three essays written in the early 1930s, towards the end of his first decade of living in China, and in three more essays written in the late 1940s just after he had left China. Teilhard had knowledge not only of China but also, through his travels, of Japan, India, Burma, and Java; he was to some extent familiar with Eastern religious thought through reading and through personal contacts. And yet, his writings show a failure to go deeply into any of the Eastern religious currents, a lack of study in depth of the basic texts, and a marked tendency to simplify by grouping all Hinduism and Buddhism under the rubric of 'Eastern religions'.[12]

Teilhard's sympathies lay not so much with Eastern

religions as with what he perceived as an underlying pantheism that finds God everywhere and in all things. He made no apologies for what he called 'my personal tendencies towards pantheism'; 'I have', he writes in his retreat journal, 'a pantheist soul.'[13] These pantheistic tendencies, innate perhaps in his temperament, accentuated by the emphasis in Jesuit spirituality on 'finding God in all things', come to theological formulation as Teilhard's doctrine of the universal influence of the risen Christ. The risen Jesus stands not only as the Omega of the world's convergent progress; he exercises an intimate influence over every part of the world – which all holds together in him.

Strict pantheism, of course, is avoided because of the doctrine of differentiating union. Christ's influence is creative, not, strictly speaking, assimilative. It makes everything to be not him but itself; that is, a thing becomes itself in being identified with him. Christ's universal influence makes things not to-be-God, but simply to-be. A creative influence, it bestows not divinity – although it divinizes that God might be all in all – but existence.

Nevertheless, the temptation to pantheism, even if successfully and clearly resisted, shows up in Teilhard's writings. He faces this temptation and copes with it by stressing the differences between an admittedly generalized Eastern pantheism and his own ideas on the unity and union between God and the world, a union in Christ moving towards an always greater unity. This, I believe, helps to explain what appears to be an over-simplification of the tenets of Eastern religions; Teilhard wants not to analyse or describe these religions for their own sake, but to use their general direction as a counterfoil for his own thought. At the same time, in doing this, he points out what, in a general way, Eastern religions have to say to Christianity to help it to be more Christian. And he arrives at some valid ecumenical principles for relationships between Christianity and the religions of the East.

Teilhard's earlier essays tend to reduce 'Eastern religions' to a kind of world-denying pantheism. In admittedly greatly oversimplified terms, the 'Eastern solution' to the problem of finding unity in the world is to see that the multiplicity of beings and desires is just a bad dream. We should awaken, suppress efforts to find knowledge and love, forget any personalization, and then – as a direct consequence of dissolving like a drop of water in the ocean, as a result of the suppression of plurality – we shall recognize the world's basic oneness. 'When silence reigns, we shall hear the single note', because 'things' in their plurality do not reveal reality – they mask it.[14] This mysticism of negation denies true reality to the 'many' in order to find unity in the 'one', in the real oneness of everything.

Psychologically, it means the suppression of human desires and drives in a withdrawal from life 'on the surface'. The means to unity is the denial and suppression of the multiple.[15] This doctrine is, logically, 'a doctrine of passivity, of relaxation of tension, of withdrawal from things – a doctrine in fact that is totally ineffective and dead.'[16]

The later essays show a more developed appreciation of the values and the differences of the great Eastern religions. Teilhard does not at all abandon his previous generalizations. He still states that in the general Eastern religious current the personal 'egos are regarded as anomalies to be reduced (or as holes to be filled up) in universal being; or, which comes to the same thing, the biological evolution of the world represents for the sage no more than an illusion or an insignificant eddy.'[17] And 'the road of the East' he describes as trying to effect spiritual unification through return to a common 'divine' basis underlying and more real than the world we apprehend through our senses.[18] However, in the longest, 'The Spiritual Contribution of the Far East', Teilhard distinguishes and compares the religions of India, China and Japan, bringing out their complementary positive aspects.[19] But he concludes that 'the East has not solved the problem of the spirit; and we would look in vain in that quarter for the dawn to illuminate it.'[20]

India can bring us to a greater awareness of both God's immanence and his transcendence; Chinese religions can help us appreciate more the material everyday world around us, and the religious traditions of Japan impress us with their sense of social loyalty. But it is only in Christianity that we find a mysticism of unity through the *unification* of the multiple. The West, contrary to the East, says, 'If you wish to become one with all reality, embrace the multiple, urge it with all your energy in the direction it already tends – to become organized and to converge.' This mysticism, writes Teilhard, 'calls for a constant effort to rise higher, to leave behind, to pass through; but it works.'[21]

'The road of the West' justifies and even hallows the value of human endeavour, gives to love its true dignity as the supreme spiritual energy, and restores the irreplaceable and incommunicable dignity of the person. In fact, and Teilhard points out what he considers already obvious, Asia looks more and more to the West precisely for many of the values inherent in its religious tradition as lived today. And he refers to Tagore's humanism, Mao's communism, and Japanese political philosophy.[22]

What about the *convergence* of East and West? This convergence will come about only on the basis of a convergence around the axis of an incarnational and future-oriented Christian spirituality. The spiritual contributions of the great traditional Eastern spiritualities will add 'volume and richness' to the new (the humano-Christian) mystical note rising from the West, but it is only in Christianity that the fundamental structure and direction of an effective world spirituality can be discovered.[23]

This means, for ecumenism, that – although Christian ecumenism ought to be one of convergence on the risen Christ – ecumenism 'between men in general' must be 'concerned to define and extend the foundations of a common human "faith" in the future of mankind.'[24] In the end, of course, faith in mankind, if taken as far as it can go, cannot be satisfied without a fully explicit faith in Jesus Christ risen.[25]

Christianity and Marxism

When discussing the great world religions besides Christianity, Teilhard does not bring Judaism into the discussion; apparently he considers the whole Judeo-Christian tradition as one great religious current. And he refers to Islam hardly at all.[26] But he understands Marxism as the codification of a religion with no revelation and with no apparent God, a sort of 'humanist pantheism'.[27] Under the heading 'An attempt at an absolute classification of religions', he gives space to Marxism. More than anti-Christian, communism is a religious competitor of Christianity.

Teilhard belonged to a generation of Jesuits that gave no study, nor even thought, to Marxism. In Paris, in 1924, he met Ida Treat, an ardent communist, an American divorced from a French communist leader. Teilhard was assigned to direct a thesis she was preparing, and they became friends.[28] Long discussions led Teilhard to study and reflect on his friend's beliefs. He never had any illusions about communism; but he admired some of its characteristics: enthusiasm for organization, devotion to progress, interest in working towards the future.

After Paris, Teilhard spent over two decades in China, travelling, leaving China only three years before Mao Tse-Tung's final victory in 1949. Teilhard always read a great deal, and he had considerable exposure to Marxist thought. His judgement of Marxism seems better grounded, both in his reading and in his life-experience, than his opinions of Eastern spiritualities.

But Teilhard's interest in Marxism confines itself for the most part to those aspects that compare and contrast with his own ideas. Not communism as a revolutionary movement of the proletariat, but Marxism as a programme for restructuring human society; not the class struggle so much as 'the whole *Movement* against Inertia'.[29] In other words, Teilhard's interest lay in what he saw as the more properly religious dimensions of Marxist doctrine and practice: the primacy of the future, faith in human progress, the sense of mankind as a whole. 'Stronger and more profound than its sense of justice, I believe that the contagious power of Marxism is its illegitimate monopolization of the *Sense of Evolution*.'[30] It is the Marxist stress on hope that interests Teilhard. Christians and communists stand together at least in so far as they both believe in the future. 'What more do they need that they may know and love one another?'[31]

In a paper for the World Congress of Faiths in 1947, Teilhard writes that the Christian and the Marxist incontestably feel a basic sympathy for one another because, even if they represent opposite poles, each is 'fundamentally inspired with an equal faith in Man'.[32] And Teilhard continues, 'Followed to their conclusion, the two paths must certainly end by coming together: for in the nature of things everything that is faith must rise, and everything that rises must converge.'[33] He writes in a letter that he absolutely refuses

> . . . to admit that atheism is an organic part of Marxism: Marxism does not deny the *whole God*, but only the God of the Above, *in the measure that* this God seems incompatible with the God of the Forward. From this, there is a way of mutual understanding between the Christian and the Marxist.[34]

At the same time, Teilhard's critique of Marxism is radical: Marxism lacks Jesus Christ risen as its present meaning and its future focus. Through the communist effort, a spirit of centred organization 'is striving to emerge'; but 'it will never succeed in doing so until the party theoreticians make up their minds at last to accord

to the superstructure of the world the ultimate consistency that they confine to the material . . .'[35] – that is a
personal Omega and all that that entails. For Teilhard,
Marxism and its expression in different forms of
communism is a caricature of true humanism. Because it
rules out the existence of a personal Centre at its
consummation, it cannot justify – or sustain – its
momentum to the end.[36]

Because Marxism lacks a personal Centre, it devalues
the personal, and it

> . . . deforms the 'person-ness' (the morality of those it
> collectivizes); in the face of Communism, the personal
> in us recoils; . . . this 'personal' is basically what is
> saved by Democracy – and there lies the true
> distinction between Communism and Democracy.[37]

A fundamental flaw of communism is that it does not
respect the integrity of the person. 'They pretend', he
writes in his notebook, 'to humanize Humanity while
dehumanizing the individual.'[38] 'Communism has come
practically to destroy the person and to make man into a
termite.'[39] Furthermore this absence of personalism
not only perverts attitudes towards human dignity
but it also reduces human progress to the mechanical
development of a soulless collectivity. 'Matter has
cast a veil over Spirit. A pseudo-determinism has killed
love.'[40]

Again because Marxism has no personal Centre
drawing it ahead into the future, it stands ultimately
doomed. 'Worldly faith in itself is not enough to move
the earth forward.'[41] Marxism does posit its own kind of
'Omega' point, but not a personal and life-giving one

that we can speak to and that can win our hearts and centre them. But unless mankind can foresee a future consonant with his own nature he will lose his taste for life, his drive to go on, his will to survive. Mankind needs a promise, a guarantee, that its evolution, its progress, the whole human enterprise, will eventually have a successful outcome. If mankind does not have this assurance, its will to move ahead will die; it will lose hope; the thrust of progress will cease. Marxism has a built-in failure mechanism; it cannot offer real hope to mankind.[42]

At its best, Marxism is a kind of truncated Christianity. Whatever it has that is good and beautiful, Christianity possesses also, and in a fuller and more coherent way. Is the Marxist committed to building the earth? So is the Christian. And if many Christians hold back, Teilhard tells the Marxist: 'Do not blame anything but our weakness; our faith imposes on us the right and the duty to throw ourselves into the things of the earth.'[43] 'You are men, you say? *Plus et ego.*'[44] And I even more.

What Christianity offers to Marxism is what it offers to all non-Christian religions: Jesus Christ, risen from the dead, God's promise to us of an ultimately successful outcome, the ground of human hope, Emmanuel – God with us and ahead of us, the God of the 'upward' and the God of the 'forward'. The fundamental principle of Teilhard's ecumenical spirituality is not really a principle but a Person.

The Centre of Teilhard de Chardin's spirituality is, at the same time, the Centre of each human life and the Centre of all history: the risen Christ of the Christian tradition and especially of the letters of Saint Paul. For

Teilhard, as for Paul, the risen Jesus stands not only as he-who-is-to-come but, precisely because he is the future focal point of all history, as mediator now between humanity and God. As Omega, he is present now and 'in him all things hold together' as he 'reconciles to himself all things' according to God's plan 'to unite all things in him' so that 'every tongue confess that Jesus Christ is Lord'.[45]

Prayer of finding all things in Jesus Christ, and him in all things

> You have so filled the universe in every direction, Jesus, that henceforth it is blessedly impossible for us to escape you. 'Where can I go to flee from your face?' Now I know for certain: neither life, whose advance increases your hold upon me; nor death, which throws me into your hands; nor the good or evil spiritual powers which are your living instruments; nor the energies of matter into which you have plunged; . . . nor the unfathomable abysses of space which are the measure of your greatness, neither death, nor life, nor angels, nor principalities, nor things present, nor things to come, nor powers, nor height, nor depth, nor any creature (Romans 8:38) – none of these things will be able to separate me from your substantial love, because they are all only the veil, the 'species', under which you take hold of me in order that I may take hold of you.
>
> Disperse, O Jesus, the clouds with your lightning! Show yourself to us as the Mighty, the Radiant, the Risen! Come to us once again as the Pantocrator who filled . . . the ancient basilicas![46]

BIBLIOGRAPHY

1 *Books by Teilhard de Chardin published in English*

ACTIVATION OF ENERGY, Collins, London, 1970, and Harper
& Row, New York, 1971

APPEARANCE OF MAN, THE, Collins, London, and Harper &
Row, New York, 1965

CHRISTIANITY AND EVOLUTION, Collins, London, and
Harcourt Brace Jovanovich Inc., New York, 1969

FUTURE OF MAN, THE, Collins, London, and Harper &
Row, New York, 1964; paperback: Fount/Fontana,
London

HEART OF MATTER, THE, Collins, London, and Harcourt
Brace Jovanovich Inc., New York, 1978

HUMAN ENERGY, Collins, London, 1969

HYMN OF THE UNIVERSE, Collins, London, and Harper &
Row, New York, 1965; paperback: Fount/Fontana,
London

LET ME EXPLAIN, edited by J. P. Demoulin; Collins, London,
and Harper & Row, New York, 1970; paperback:
Fount/Fontana, London

LETTERS FROM A TRAVELLER, Collins, London, and Harper
& Row, New York, 1962; paperback: Fount/Fontana,
London

LETTERS TO LÉONTINE ZANTA, Collins, London, 1969

LETTERS TO TWO FRIENDS, The New American Library,
New York, 1968; Fontana Library of Theology and
Philosophy, London, 1972

MAKING OF A MIND, THE, Collins, London, and Harper &
Row, New York, 1965

MAN'S PLACE IN NATURE, Collins, London, and Harper &
Row, New York, 1966; paperback: Fount/Fontana,
London

Bibliography

MILIEU DIVIN, LE, Collins, London, and (as THE DIVINE MILIEU) Harper & Row, New York, 1960; paperback: Fount/Fontana, London

ON HAPPINESS, Collins, London, 1973

ON SUFFERING, Collins, London, 1975

PHENOMENON OF MAN, THE, Collins, London, and Harper & Brothers, New York, 1959; paperback:Fount/Fontana, London

PRAYER OF THE UNIVERSE, THE (Selection from WRITINGS IN TIME OF WAR), Fontana Books, London, 1973

SCIENCE AND CHRIST, Collins, London, and Harper & Row, New York, 1968

TOWARD THE FUTURE, Collins, London, and Harcourt Brace Jovanovich Inc., New York, 1975

VISION OF THE PAST, THE, Collins, London, and Harper & Row, New York, 1966

WRITINGS IN TIME OF WAR, Collins, London, and Harper & Row, New York, 1968

2 Some books about Teilhard de Chardin and his thought

SPIRITUALITY OF TEILHARD DE CHARDIN, THE, by Thomas Corbishley; Fontana Library of Theology and Philosophy, London, 1971

TEILHARD DE CHARDIN: A BIOGRAPHICAL STUDY, by Claude Cuénot; Burns Oates, London, and Helican Press, Inc., Baltimore, 1965

EVOLUTION, THE THEORY OF TEILHARD DE CHARDIN, by Bernard Delfgaauw; Fontana Library of Theology and Philosophy, London, and Harper & Row, New York, 1969

TOWARDS A NEW MYSTICISM, by Ursula King; Collins, London, 1980 and Seabury Press, New York, 1981

ETERNAL FEMININE, THE, by Henri de Lubac; Collins, London, and Harper & Row, New York, 1971

RELIGION OF TEILHARD DE CHARDIN, THE, by Henri de Lubac; Collins, London, and Desclée Co. Inc., New York, 1967

Bibliography

TEILHARD – A BIOGRAPHY, by Mary and Ellen Lukas; Collins, London, and Doubleday & Co. Inc., New York, 1977

TEILHARD DE CHARDIN AND THE MYSTERY OF CHRIST, by Christopher Mooney; Collins, London, and Harper & Row, New York, 1966

TEILHARD DE CHARDIN ALBUM, by Jeanne Mortier and Marie-Louise Aboux; Collins, London, and Harper & Row, New York, 1966

TEILHARD DE CHARDIN: SCIENTIST AND SEER, by C. E. Raven; Collins, London, and Harper & Row, New York, 1962

TEILHARD DE CHARDIN: A GUIDE TO HIS THOUGHT, by Emile Rideau; Collins, London, 1967

TEILHARD DE CHARDIN: A BIOGRAPHY, by Robert Speaight; Collins, London, 1967

MEMORIES OF TEILHARD DE CHARDIN, by Helmut de Terra; Collins, London, and Harper & Row, New York, 1964

CONCERNING TEILHARD: AND OTHER WRITINGS ON SCIENCE AND RELIGION, by Bernard Towers; Collins, London, 1969

INTRODUCTION TO TEILHARD DE CHARDIN, AN, by N. M. Wildiers; Fontana Books, London, and Harper & Row, New York, 1968

HUMAN SEARCH, THE, by George Appleton, Michael Le Morvan, John Newson and Melvyn Thompson; Fount Paperbacks, London, 1979

TEILHARD DE CHARDIN'S THEOLOGY OF THE CHRISTIAN IN THE WORLD, by Robert Faricy; Sheed & Ward, New York, 1967

NOTES

Chapter One

1 Cahier F, 17 October 1919, quoted in P. Schellenbaum, *Le Christ dans l'énergetique Teilhardienne* (Paris: 1971), p. 192. Schellenbaum, in his section on the Sacred Heart (pp. 185–200), shows clearly how Teilhard's whole conception of the relationship between nature and grace, including his particular understanding of grace as transforming nature, has its origin in Teilhard's devotion to the Sacred Heart.

This chapter has been published, in a different form, in *The Teilhard Review*, 13 (1978), pp. 82–8.

2 'The Heart of Matter', in *The Heart of Matter*, translated by René Hague, pp. 52–3.

3 Letter of 4 June 1915, to Berthe Teilhard de Chardin, quoted in Schellenbaum, *op. cit.*, p. 187.

4 Letter of 2 July 1915, to Berthe Teilhard de Chardin, quoted in *ibid.*, p. 187.

5 Letter of 9 December 1915, to Berthe Teilhard de Chardin, quoted in *ibid.*, p. 188.

6 Letter of 9 February 1916, to Berthe Teilhard de Chardin, quoted in *ibid.*, pp. 188–9.

7 Letters of 28 June and 8 July 1916, to Berthe Teilhard de Chardin, quoted in *ibid.*, p. 189.

8 Letter of 13 June 1917, to Berthe Teilhard de Chardin, quoted in *ibid.*, p. 190.

9 *Ibid.*

10 Unpublished retreat notes, 1939–43.

11 *Ibid.*, 1943 retreat, first day; see his more nuanced remarks for publication in the 1940 essay, 'The Awaited Word', in *Toward the Future*, translated by René Hague, pp. 98–9.

12 *Ibid.*, 1940 retreat, eight day.

13 Unpublished retreat notes, 1944–53, 1948 retreat, fifth, sixth, and seventh days.

14 The litany is published at the end of the collection of his essays entitled *Christianity and Evolution*, translated by René Hague, pp. 244–5.

15 *Ibid.*

16 Unpublished retreat notes, 1944–53, 1950 retreat, sixth and seventh days.

17 *Ibid.*, 1945 retreat, sixth day.

18 *Ibid.*, 1950 retreat, ninth day.

19 Unpublished retreat notes, 1939–43, 1943 retreat, first day.

20 Unpublished retreat notes, 1944–53, 1944 retreat, fifth day.

21 Journal number 6, p. 106, quoted in P. Wienisch, *Teilhard de Chardin et la dévotion au Sacré-Coeur, Paray le Monial*, 11, no. 11 (1976), p. 25.

22 *Ibid.*, p. 112, quoted in *ibid.*, p. 25.

23 *Ibid.*

24 'The Awaited Word', in *Toward the Future*, p. 98.

25 'The Heart of Matter', in *The Heart of Matter*, p. 16.

26 *Ibid.*, pp. 42–3.

27 *Ibid.*, pp. 45–9.

28 *Ibid.*, p. 44.

29 *Ibid.*, p. 41.

30 *Ibid.*, pp. 41–3.

31 *Ibid.*, p. 43 (my translation).

32 *Ibid.*, pp. 43–4.

33 *Ibid.*, p. 47.

34 *Ibid.* (my translation).

35 Letter of 4 August 1916, in *The Making of a Mind*, translated by René Hague, p. 181.

36 *Le Milieu Divin*, translated by B. Wall *et al.*, p. 144.

37 'The Spirit of the Earth', in *Human Energy*, translated by J. M. Cohen, pp. 32–6.

38 This three-stage analysis of human love is found in 'Sketch of a Personalistic Universe', in *Human Energy*, pp. 53–92.

39 'Human Energy', in *Human Energy*, pp. 145–55; see also *The Phenomenon of Man*, translated by B. Wall, revised translation (New York: 1965), pp. 264–9 and 295–6.

40 'Human Energy', pp. 156–8.

41 'Life and the Planets', in *The Future of Man*, translated by H. Denny, pp. 118–19.

42 *The Phenomenon of Man*, p. 263.

43 'The Directions and Conditions of the Future', in *The Future of Man*, p. 235; see 'Centrology', in *The Activation of Energy*, translated by René Hague, pp. 116–17.

44 Quoted in Joseph Needham, 'Love Sacred and Profane', *Theology*, 80 (1977), p. 16.

45 These ideas are brought out in two essays written in 1950: 'How May We Conceive and Hope that Human Unanimization Will Be Realized on Earth?' in *The Future of Man*, pp. 286–9; and 'On the Probable Coming of an Ultra-Humanity', in *ibid.*, pp. 277–80.

46 'The Singularities of the Human Species', in *The Appearance of Man*, translated by J. M. Cohen, p. 273.

47 Unpublished retreat notes, 1939–43, 1940 retreat, eighth day.

48 See 'The Heart of Matter', in *The Heart of Matter*, pp. 49–58.

49 See 'The Christic', in *The Heart of Matter*, p. 88.

50 'Super-Humanity, Super-Christ, Super-Charity', in *Science and Christ*, translated by René Hague, p. 169.

51 *Ibid.*, p. 170.

52 'Pantheism and Christianity', in *Christianity and Evolution*, p. 73.

53 *Ibid.*, pp. 73–4

54 'My Universe', in *Science and Christ*, p. 65.

55 *Ibid.*

56 *Ibid.*

57 *Le Milieu Divin*, pp. 123–4.

58 'The Christic', in *The Heart of Matter*, p. 94. See the essays, 'The Priest' and *Forma Christi*, in *Writings in Time of War*, translated by René Hague, pp. 203–24

and 249–70; also, the beautifully prayerful essays of *Hymn of the Universe*, translated by S. Bartholomew.

59 *Hymn of the Universe*, pp. 41–55.

60 *Ibid.*, p. 43.

61 'The Mass on the World', in *Hymn of the Universe*, p. 32.

62 *Le Milieu Divin*, pp. 145–6.

Chapter Two

1   See 'Some Reflections on the Conversion of the World', in *Science and Christ*, pp. 122–3; and *'La pensée du Père Teilhard de Chardin'*, *Les études philosophiques*, 10 (1955), pp. 580–1, a short article written by Teilhard himself.

2   Both essays are in *Writings in Time of War*, pp, 13–71 and 75–91.

3   'Cosmic Life', in *Writings in Time of War*, p. 57.

4   'Mastery of the World and the Kingdom of God', in *Writings in Time of War*, p. 87. See also, 'A Note on Progress', in *The Future of Man*, pp. 11–24.

5   *Op. cit.*, pp. 50–3.

6   'The Priest', in *Writings in Time of War*, pp. 205–24; *'Forma Christi'*, in *ibid.*, pp. 250–69; 'The Mass on the World', in *Hymn of the Universe*, pp. 19–37.

7   See especially, 'The Sense of Man', in *Toward the Future*, pp. 13–39; and 'The Road of the West', in *ibid.*, pp. 40–59.

8   'Sketch of a Personalistic Universe', in *Human Energy*, pp. 53–92.

9   'Christianity in the World', in *Science and Christ*, pp. 98–112.

10 'Christianity and Evolution', in *Christianity and Evolution*, p. 174.

11 'Some Reflections on the Conversion of the World', in *Science and Christ*, pp. 118–20.

12 See, for example, 'The Phenomenon of Spirituality', in

Notes

Human Energy, pp. 93–112; and 'Sketch of a Personalistic Universe', in *ibid.*, pp. 53–92.

13 See, for example, 'Some General Views on the Essence of Christianity', in *Christianity and Evolution*, pp. 133–7; 'Christ the Evolver', in *ibid.*, pp. 138–50; 'Introduction to the Christian Life', in *ibid.*, pp. 151–72; and 'Super-Humanity, Super-Christ, Super-Charity', in *Science and Christ*, pp. 151–73.

14 *Toward the Future*, pp. 92–100 and 101–6.

15 *Ibid.*, p. 103. See the profound and exact analysis of Teilhard's idea of the relationship between the natural and the supernatural in H. de Lubac, *The Eternal Feminine*, translated by René Hague, pp. 77–84. See also B. de Solages, *Teilhard de Chardin* (Paris: 1967), pp. 296–305.

16 *Toward The Future*, p. 105.

17 Philippians 2:7–8.

18 See Ephesians 4:9–10.

19 *Toward The Future*, p. 106.

20 What does Teilhard mean by 'the material'? At times in his writings the word 'material' (or 'matter') is used in a more or less metaphysical sense to mean 'multiplicity' or 'the multiple'. At other times, as in *Le Milieu Divin*, 'the material' means the material world taken in its concrete materiality. In 'A Note on the Concept of Christian Perfection' (in *Toward the Future*, pp. 101–6), 'the material' seems to stand for the material world, in accord with the second meaning. But the connotation of multiplicity is nevertheless present. This is also the way the term 'the material' is used in this chapter.

21 'A Note on the Concept of Christian Perfection', in *Toward the Future*, p. 106.

22 In *Christianity and Evolution*, p. 107.

23 See 'The Death-Barrier and Co-Reflection', in *Activation of Energy*, pp. 397–406.

24 'The Heart of the Problem', in *The Future of Man*, pp. 260–9.

25 'The Basis of My Attitude', in *The Heart of Matter*, p. 147.

26 J. Laberge has reproduced Teilhard's 1922 retreat notes in the Appendix of *Pierre Teilhard de Chardin et Ignace de Loyola* (Paris: 1973), pp. 227–35; the quotation is from pp. 233–4. All Teilhard's other retreat notes are either unpublished, or, in the case of many of his years in China up to 1940, lost.

27 Unpublished retreat notes, 1939–43, 1943 retreat, eighth day.

28 Unpublished retreat notes, 1944–53, 1945 retreat, eighth day.

29 Unpublished retreat notes, 1954 retreat, eighth day.

30 'Cosmic Life', in *Writings in Time of War*, pp. 69–70.

Chapter Three

1 The term is not a regular part of Teilhard's theological vocabulary since, in the Catholic theology of his time, it referred only to the study of the 'four last things': death, purgatory, heaven, hell. Contemporary theology, however, has greatly broadened the concept of eschatology.

2 *Contra Julianum*, I, 9, 42.

3 *Sent.*, d. 34, a. 1 and 2; *Summa theologiae*, Ia, q. 48, a. 1 and 3; *Contra gentiles*, 1. III, c. 6 and 7; *De malo*, q. 1, a. 1.

4 'Introductory Statement', section 4, in *The Documents of Vatican II*, ed. W. Abbott (America Press, New York, Geoffrey Chapman, London, 1966), p. 200.

5 *Ibid.*

6 *Ibid.*, section 39, p. 237.

7 *Ibid.*, section 45, p. 247.

8 For Teilhard's theology of evil, see especially 'Christology and Evolution', in *Christianity and Evolution*, pp. 84–93; 'Reflections on Original Sin', in *ibid.*, pp. 187–98; 'Christ the Evolver', in *ibid.*, pp. 148–50;

Notes

'Fall, Redemption, and Geocentrism', in *ibid.*, pp. 36–44; and 'Note on Some Possible Historical Representations of Original Sin', in *ibid.*, pp. 45–55.

9 '*La pensée de Père Teilhard de Chardin*', *Les études philosophiques*, 10 (1955), p. 581.

10 *The Phenomenon of Man*, p. 313.

11 See the references in footnote 8 of this chapter for Teilhard's chief writings on original sin.

12 This literature includes: P. Schoonenberg, *God's World in the Making* (Pittsburgh: 1964); and *Man and Sin*, translated by J. Donceel (Notre Dame: 1965); S. Trooster, *Evolution and the Doctrine of Original Sin* (New York: 1968); and many other books and articles.

13 See *Le Milieu Divin*, especially pp. 66–70 and 96.

14 'The Phenomenon of Spirituality', in *Human Energy*, p. 106.

15 *Theology of Liberation*, translated by C. Inda and J. Eagleson (New York: 1973), pp. 173–5. The bibliography on Latin American theology of liberation would fill several books. A good survey is: P. Berryman, 'Latin American Liberation Theology', *Theological Studies*, 34 (1973), pp. 357–95. See also Segundo Galilea, '*Théologie de la libération*', *Lumen Vitae*, 33 (1978), pp. 205–28; *Pro Mundi Vita* for March-April, 1978 ('The Churches of Latin America in Confrontation with the State and the Ideology of National Security'); *Concilium*, 6 (1974) has several articles on theology of liberation, notably two by G. Gutierrez and L. Boff; *Theology Digest*, 23 (1975), contains an excellent survey of liberation theology; *Nouvelle revue théologique*, 89 (1976), has a good evaluative article by P. André-Vincent, '*Les théologies de la libération*', pp. 109–25.

16 C. Strain, 'Ideology and Alienation: Theses on the Interpretation and Evaluation of Theologies of Liberation', *Journal of the American Academy of Religion*, 45 (1977), pp. 473–90. See also, however, Segundo Galilea, 'Liberation as an Encounter with

Politics and Contemplation', *Concilium*, 6 (1974), pp. 19–33.

17 See, for example, Exodus 3:7–8 and 13:3; Isaiah 43:16 and 61:1.

18 See Luke 24:21; Matthew 1:21 and 20:28; John 8:32; Galatians 5:1.

19 Judges 1:18. See Genesis 4:13, 21:16–20; Judges 15:18–19, 21:2; I Samuel 1:10–20, 12:6–17; 2 Chronicles 6:24–31; Job 42:1–6 and 10; these are all cases of individual persons crying out to God. See the following texts for laments for the suffering of the people, laments that cry out for the people's deliverance: Psalms 79 and 80; Isaiah 63:15–64:12; Judges 6:13–16; Exodus 32:11–14, 32:30–32, 33:12–19; Deuteronomy 9:25–29; Numbers 11:1–23, 14:11–19; Joshua 7:6–9; 2 Samuel 24:17; Judith chapter 9; Daniel 9:3–19; Ezra chapter 9; Nehemiah 9:6–38; Lamentations, especially the last chapter, 5:16–22. See also Luke 18:1–8, 13:34–35, 21:23.

20 Revelation 1:8.

21 Revelation 22:13.

22 Matthew 25:31.

23 Unpublished retreat notes, 1939–43, 1939 retreat, fifth day.

24 Unpublished retreat notes, 1944–53, 1944 retreat, eighth day.

25 *Dieu et l'utopie* (Paris: 1977), p. 19 and *passim*.

26 *On Not Leaving It to the Snake* (New York: 1967), pp. 35–7.

27 'The Hermeneutics of Eschatological Assertions', in *Theological Investigations*, vol. 4 (New York: 1966), p. 337.

28 *Le Milieu Divin*, pp. 147–9.

29 See Ewert Cousins, 'Teilhard and the Theology of the Spirit', *Cross Currents*, 19 (1959), pp. 159–77.

30 *Le Milieu Divin*, pp. 147–9.

Notes

Chapter Four

1 *Op. cit.* The present chapter has been published in a slightly different form in *Horizons*, 3 (1976), pp. 1–16; and in *The Cross Today*, by G. O'Collins, R. Faricy, and M. Flick (Rome, Sydney and New York: 1977), pp. 12–29.

2 Revelation 21:4.

3 While reading W. Somerset Maugham's *The Razor's Edge*, Teilhard copied a few lines into a notebook he kept for his reading notes: 'I wanted to believe, but I could not believe in a god which was not better than the ordinary decent man' (unpublished reading notes, notebook II for 1945, p. 58). For Teilhard, Christ is, while completely human, still – in a certain sense – as big as the world, because he is its Keystone and its Prime Mover ('The Christic', in *The Heart of Matter*, p. 94); Teilhard believed that this is the God contemporary man is looking for.

4 'The Sense of Man', in *Toward the Future*, p. 34.

5 'The Road of the West', in *Toward the Future*, p. 53.

6 'My Universe', in *Science and Christ*, pp. 60–1.

7 'Christology and Evolution', in *Christianity and Evolution*, p. 85.

8 *Journal*, vol 1 (26 August 1916 – 4 January 1919), complete text published by N. and K. Schmitz-Moormann (Paris: 1975), p. 68.

9 *Ibid.*, p. 82.

10 'Introduction to the Christian Life', in *Christianity and Evolution*, p. 163.

11 'Christianity and Evolution', in *Christianity and Evolution*, p. 181.

12 Unpublished letter, 11 August 1936.

13 Unpublished letter of 21 May 1952, to François Richaud. Teilhard goes on to say that he 'absolutely refuses to admit that atheism is an organic part of Marxism: Marxism does not deny the *whole God*, but only the

God of the Above, *in the measure that* this God seems incompatible with the God of the Forward. From this, there is a way of mutual understanding between the Christian and the Marxist *in the perspective* of a universe in a state of cosmogenesis (but only in such a universe).'

14 *Journal*, p. 190.
15 'The Struggle Against the Multitude', in *Writings in Time of War*, translated by René Hague, p. 107.
16 'Cosmic Life', in *Writings in Time of War*, p. 67.
17 'Introduction to the Christian Life', p. 163.
18 *Idem.*
19 *Le Milieu Divin*, translated by B. Wall *et al.*, pp. 101–4.
20 *Ibid.*, pp. 103–4.
21 *Ibid.*, p. 104.
22 In *Christianity and Evolution*, pp. 212–20.
23 *Ibid.*, p. 216.
24 Letter of 18 September 1948, to Rhoda de Terra, published in *Letters to Two Friends*, p. 187.
25 Unpublished retreat notes, 1939–43, 1941 retreat.
26 *Ibid.*
27 *Ibid.*, 1942 retreat.
28 Letter of Good Friday, 1955, to Father Ravier, in *Pierre Teilhard de Chardin: Lettres intimes*, ed. H. de Lubac (Paris: 1972), pp. 465–6.
29 These three phases of Christian personalization, which form the outline of much of *Le Milieu Divin*, are to be found outlined concisely in the essay 'Reflections on Happiness', in *Toward the Future*, pp. 117–20.
30 *Le Milieu Divin*, p. 96.
31 *Ibid.*, p. 97.
32 H. de Lubac, '*Maurice Blondel et le Père Teilhard de Chardin, mémoires échangés en décembre 1919, présentés par H. de Lubac*', *Archives de philosophie*, 24 (1961), pp. 123–56.
33 Notes from public debate, 21 January 1947, Paris; unpublished.
34 *The Phenomenon of Man*, p. 312.

35 'Operative Faith', in *Writings in Time of War*, p. 230.
36 *Journal*, p. 337; cf. pp. 164–7 and 183.
37 'My Universe', in *Science and Christ*, p. 62.
38 *Ibid.*, p. 63.
39 *Le Milieu Divin*, p. 88.
40 See Laberge, *op. cit.*, pp. 165–73.
41 Unpublished retreat notes, 1939–43, 1939 retreat.
42 *Ibid.*, 1941 retreat.
43 *Ibid.*, 1943 retreat.
44 *Ibid.*, 1942 retreat.
45 *Ibid.*, 1939 retreat.
46 *Ibid.*, 1941 retreat.
47 *Ibid.*, 1942 retreat.
48 Unpublished retreat notes, 1944–53, 1945 retreat.
49 *Ibid.*
50 *Ibid.*, 1949 retreat.
51 Letter of 16 February 1953, quoted in *Pierre Teilhard de Chardin: Lettres intimes*, p. 401, footnote 6.
52 Letter of 25 January 1950, quoted in *ibid.*
53 Unpublished retreat notes, 1944–53, 1944 retreat.
54 *Ibid.*
55 *Ibid.*, 1945 retreat.
56 *Ibid.*, 1946 retreat.
57 *Ibid.*, 1948 retreat.
58 Unpublished retreat notes, 1954 retreat.
59 *Le Milieu Divin*, pp. 89–90.

Chapter Five

1 Section 3, in *The Documents of Vatican II*, ed. W. Abbott (America Press, New York, Geoffrey Chapman, London, 1966), p. 345. Cf. also *Lumen Gentium*, section 15, in *ibid.*, pp. 33–4.
2 Teilhard's ideas on the Church are scattered. See especially: 'Introduction to the Christian Life', in *Christianity and Evolution*, translated by René Hague, pp. 151–7 and 167–8; and 'Turmoil or Genesis?' in *The*

Future of Man, translated by N. Denny, pp. 223–5.

3 Cf. *Lumen Gentium*, sections 48–51, in *The Documents of Vatican II, op. cit.*, pp. 78–85.

4 'Introduction to the Christian Life', in *Christianity and Evolution*, p. 168.

5 'The Zest for Living', in *Activation of Energy*, translated by René Hague, p. 241, footnote

6 'Ecumenism', in *Science and Christ*, translated by René Hague, pp. 197–8.

7 'Drawn and Held Together', *The Ecumenical Review*, 26 (1974), p. 172.

8 Cf. *passim* in the writings of Teilhard, and especially 'The Grand Option', in *The Future of Man*, pp. 52–7.

9 'Ecumenism', in *Science and Christ*, p. 197.

10 *Journal* no. 8, unpublished, p. 79, entry for 31 July 1954; the original is: rapports: L'oecuménisme
$$\text{rapports:}\quad \text{L'oecuménisme} \left(\begin{array}{l} \text{common ground} \\ \text{versus axe de convergence.} \end{array} \right)$$

11 'Ecumenism', in *Science and Christ*, p. 197. For an excellent and thorough study of Teilhard in reference to Eastern religions, see Ursula King, *Towards a New Mysticism* (1980).

12 Ursula King has pointed this out clearly; see her article, 'Teilhard's Comparison of Eastern and Western Mysticism', *The Teilhard Review*, 10 (1975', pp. 9–16.

13 'Sketch of a Personalistic Universe', in *Human Energy*, p. 91; unpublished retreat notes, 1944–53, 1945 retreat, sixth day. And so Teilhard can speak of Christ 'mystically assimilating . . . all that surrounds him' (*Science and Christ*, p. 65), but strongly qualifies the statements.

14 'The Road of the West' (written in 1932), in *Toward the Future*, p. 43.

15 'How I Believe' (written in 1934), in *Christianity and Evolution*, p. 122.

16 'Christianity in the World' (written in 1933), in *Science and Christ*, pp. 105–6.

17 'Two Converse Forms of the Spirit' (written in 1950), in *Activation of Energy*, p. 224; cf. 'Ecumenism' (written in 1946), in *Science and Christ*, p. 197.

18 'My Fundamental Vision' (written in 1948), in *Toward the Future*, p. 200.

19 'The Spiritual Contribution of the Far East' (written in 1947), in *Toward the Future*, pp. 134–47.

20 *Ibid.*, p. 141.

21 *Ibid.*, p. 142.

22 *Ibid.*, pp. 144–5; see Ursula King, 'The One and the Many: The Individual and the Community from the Religious Perspective', *The Teilhard Review*, 11 (1976), pp. 9–15.

23 *Ibid.*, pp. 146–7.

24 'Ecumenism', in *Science and Christ*, p. 198.

25 *Ibid.*

26 See, however, 'Christianity in the World', in *Science and Christ*, pp. 104–5.

27 'How I Believe', in *Christianity and Evolution*, p. 123; see 'Two Converse Forms of Spirit', in *Activation of Energy*, p. 225.

28 See Pierre-Louis Mathieu, *La pensée politique et économique de Teilhard de Chardin* (Paris: 1969), pp. 54–5; Mathieu has an interesting section on '*Teilhard juge de Marx*', pp. 52–98; this is to date the fullest study of Teilhard's attitudes towards Marxism. Probably the best study of Teilhard's mentions of Marxism in his writings is, however, to be found in Joseph A. Grau, *Morality and the Human Future in the Thought of Teilhard de Chardin* (London: 1976), pp. 219–37.

29 Personal reading notes, quoted in Mathieu, *op. cit.*, p. 83.

30 Letter of 25 March 1954, to Claude Cuénot, quoted in Mathieu, *op. cit.*, p. 69.

31 'Some Reflections on Progress', in *The Future of Man*, p. 80; see 'The Planetization of Mankind', in *ibid.*, p. 139.

32 'Faith in Man', in *The Future of Man*, p. 191.

33 *Ibid.*, p. 192.

34 Unpublished letter of 21 May 1952, to François Richaud.
35 'Two Converse Forms of the Spirit', in *Activation of Energy*, p. 225.
36 'The Heart of the Problem', in *The Future of Man*, pp. 264–5.
37 Personal notes, 2 October 1945, quoted in Mathieu, *op. cit.*, p. 89; Teilhard, writing in French, uses the English word 'recoils'.
38 Personal notes, 2 June 1946, quoted in Mathieu, *op. cit.*, p. 91.
39 'The Salvation of Mankind', in *Science and Christ*, p. 140.
40 *Ibid.*
41 'The Heart of the Problem', in *The Future of Man*, p. 265.
42 This argument is developed by Teilhard in several places in his writings; see especially: *Man's Place in Nature*, translated by René Hague, pp. 115–21; 'The Directions and Conditions of the Future', in *The Future of Man*, pp. 227–37; and 'The Zest for Living', in *Activation of Energy*, pp. 229–44.
43 *Le Milieu Divin*, p. 69.
44 *Ibid.*, p. 70; see 'Research, Work and Worship', in *Science and Christ*, p. 218.
45 Colossians 1:17 and 20; Ephesians 1:10; Philippians 2:11. In support of this theology of Christ as Omega, Teilhard refers specifically to the following texts: Romans 8:18ff, 14:7–9; 1 Corinthians 4:22, 6:15ff, 10:16, 12:12ff, 15:23–29 and 39ff; 2 Corinthians 3:18, 5:11, 4 and 19; Galatians 3:27–28; Ephesians 1:10, 19–23, 2:5, 10–14, 3:6, 18, 4:9, 12:3–16; Philippians 2:10, 3:10–11, 20–21; Colossians 1:15–20 and 28, 2:9–12 and 19, 3:10; 1 Thessalonians 4:17; Hebrews 2:7–8.
46 *Le Milieu Divin*, pp. 127–8.